FROM THE GAZALA LINE TO BEHIND THE LINES

Wartime memories of John Cowtan

I.W.T.

Transcribed and edited by Jane Meredith

AuthorHouse™ UK Ltd.
500 Avebury Boulevard
Central Milton Keynes, MK9 2BE
www.authorhouse.co.uk
Phone: 08001974150

© 2011 I.W.T. All rights reserved.

No part of this book may be reproduced, stored in a retrieval system, or
transmitted by any means without the written permission of the author.

First published by AuthorHouse   7/1/2011

ISBN: 978-1-4567-7760-9 (sc)

This book is printed on acid-free paper.

Because of the dynamic nature of the Internet, any web addresses or links contained in
this book may have changed since publication and may no longer be valid. The views
expressed in this work are solely those of the author and do not necessarily reflect the
views of the publisher, and the publisher hereby disclaims any responsibility for them.

**To our great and grand parents
John and Rose Cowtan.**
Also to Pete and all the family
who have spent many an hour
with a glass of red infuriator
listening to these stories.

Contents

FOREWORD	vii
PART ONE	
EARLY DAYS	ix
CHAPTER 1 – WOOLWICH TO WAR	1
CHAPTER 2 – FRANCE	3
CHAPTER 3 – BACK IN ENGLAND	7
CHAPTER 4 – LIVERPOOL TO AFRICA	12
CHAPTER 5 – CYPRUS	18
CHAPTER 6 - PALESTINE	23
CHAPTER 7 – LIFE IN THE DESERT	25
CHAPTER 8 – GAZALA LINE	30
CHAPTER 9 - CAPTURE	41
PART 2	
ESCAPE FROM DURANCE VILE	**45**
CHAPTER 10 – PRISONER OF WAR	47
CHAPTER 11 – SEWER RATS	55
CHAPTER 12 – RELIEF FROM THE DAILY GRIND	62
CHAPTER 13 – THE LAST BRICK	65
CHAPTER 14 – JOURNEY TO BOLOGNA	75
CHAPTER 15 – ESCAPE AT LAST	82

CHAPTER 16 – INTO THE COUNTRYSIDE	89
CHAPTER 17 – PARTISANS, PRIESTS AND RAIDS	95
CHAPTER 18 - ITALIAN HOSPITALITY	105
CHAPTER 19 - SABOTAGE BEHIND THE LINES	109
APPENDIX I: Mussolini	117
APPENDIX II: Interview by Peter Liddell	121
APPENDIX III: Citations	145
ACKNOWLEDGEMENTS	147

FOREWORD

"This letter was received just before Christmas 2009. All the family were gathered together and I presented my father with an unedited copy of his manuscript for his Christmas present. Skye read out this correspondence from James McBride. Dad was very moved and touched by these words. He died exactly one week later."

Dear Major General Cowtan:

I was delighted to read your letter and hear the news of your survival in Italy during our last Good War. It is interesting to note that all of the American soldiers I interviewed had great respect for their British counterparts. Indeed the general feeling among the soldiers who served in Italy seemed to be that the British and Germans were the more disciplined soldiers, the Americans had more firepower and supplies, the Brazilians were good soldiers but not liked much by the Americans, the Gurkas were feared by all - the rumor among Americans was that the British kept them in cages during the day and let them out at night, though many Gurkas apparently died of tuberculosis over there. The Russian, Ukranians, Poles, Italian partisans and civilians ranged in from "can't be trusted" to "extraordinarily brave and clever." I'm not sure if that squares with your experience.

It is a small miracle that you survived your ordeal. Only a person who has walked through the dark and uncold certainty of the Italian Apennines can understand the severity of your situation as a soldier trying to get back across the Gothic Line, which was bad business indeed. You also happened to land in the thick of the 92nd's assault which began with light forces near Pietrasanta and Livorno that August followed by a division strength assault by the time October rolled around and you and your men were dodging death. As you know, that land is harsh, rocky, cold, nearly impossible to traverse at night unless, of course, your life is on the line, as was apparently the case here. The chaos of that campaign is described clearly in your letter. Again, only those who were there would understand the naked terror that accompanies that chaos, where you're sipping a bottle of wine one minute, and five minutes later while walking down the road looking for shelter, the Germans strafe the road and mountains with a .88. It was tight, tough work, and I'm glad you survived it.

In real life, a British unit discovered St. Anna right after the Germans massacred the town. A joint British-American tribunal was held, and inconclusive evidence drawn. I suspect no one has ever paid for that awful atrocity.

Well, I will sign off here. Thank you for serving your country and mine. Thank you for surviving the war. And finally, thank you for helping to pave the way so that I and millions like myself can enjoy the relative charm and privilege that free societies still offer in abundance. There is nothing like hearing from a veteran like yourself who was actually there.

It is an honor to hear from you, and God willing, either in this life or the next, I hope to earn the honor of shaking your hand.

May God bless you and your family in this holiday season.

With admiration,

James McBride
Author of Miracle at St. Anna

PART ONE

EARLY DAYS

CHAPTER 1 – WOOLWICH TO WAR

Before World War 2 future officers of the Royal Engineers, the Royal Artillery and the Royal Corps of Signals as it was then known, were trained as gentleman cadets at the RMA Woolwich, known as "The Shop". This training lasted 18 months, divided into 3 terms of 6 months each. At the end of 1937 and the beginning of 1938 when it appeared that World War 2 was imminent it was decided that the people in the middle term would be commissioned 6 months early thereby doing a total of only one year at The Shop instead of the full year and a half. So in July 1939, which was the year the War started, the people who had only done 2 terms were commissioned on the 3rd of July. Those who had done their full stint of 3 terms were commissioned two days earlier, and thus became senior to them in the army list. As a matter of interest, our commandant at the time was Major-General Philip Neame, V.C, which he won in WW1, and our adjutant was Major Bob Mansergh, R.H.A, who became the Master Gunner at some later date.

There were 18 commissioned to the Sappers in both of the two batches I've mentioned, so the 36 of us were almost exact contemporaries and we were sent off to the School of Military Engineering at Chatham to learn something about Royal Engineering. The 36 of us were all brought up together, and we made our friends, particular friends, indeed many of them lifelong friends, during those early days.

If the war hadn't happened, we would have expected as RE officers to do a full two years at Cambridge University taking a Mechanical Science degree, but because of the war this didn't happen. So for us 36, our future specialist academic training or university degree training was to come to most people at some later date.

Really all the basic professional training we got before being allotted to units in the regular army was the short time that we had learning basic sappery at Chatham, and that really only lasted about 6 or 8 months before we were sent off to do something else. The other thing that was notable about our early training was that we were really not taught anything about soldiers at all. We were taught about high standards of behaviour and officer-like qualities at Woolwich. We learnt a good deal of detail about field engineering and how to construct trenches, build bridges and do demolitions at Chatham, but nobody really told us much about soldiers at all and so later on when we joined our units - and it wasn't much later on at that - we were given command of various numbers of soldiers without really having been told too much about how to handle them, poor devils!

But we got on with it, and I think most of us did our first posting in training battalions which were scattered around the country. New R.E. recruits were sent to places like Newark and Elgin and formed into companies and platoons, given basic training in soldiery, in drill on the square, in shooting rifles and fixing bayonets, physical training and that sort of thing, before being posted to units in the Field Army. So we went with them and we were separately posted to units in the Field Army, or most of us were, from these training battalions.

Of course, before that on 3rd September, 1939, war had been declared and there was the extraordinary period of the phoney war over the autumn and winter of 1939/1940 while we were doing our early training. So nobody, or practically nobody, was sent to a field unit that had any fighting to do until the early months of 1940 from March onwards.

CHAPTER 2 – FRANCE

I was sent with a bunch of Sapper officer reinforcements to France in April, 1940. We went in HM ships to Le Havre, and then by train up the line to a place called Forges-les-Eaux in Normandy, where there was a Reinforcement Base Depot. We stayed in what then seemed to be a ghastly place for a week or two until the enemy did break through into Belgium and Holland in April, 1940. At that stage we were expecting to be sent as reinforcements to units that had suffered casualties but this was not to be. We were formed into what you might call an infantry battalion consisting entirely of R.E., officered by R.E and manned by Sapper other ranks.

Our commanding officer was a colourful personality called Lt. Col. Lancelot Perowne R.E., who sported a Kaiser Wilhelm moustache. I was made adjutant of this extraordinary unit called Perowne's Rifles R.E. I found one of my main tasks was to ensure that my commanding officer had sufficient pomade to keep the ends of his moustache pointing vertically upwards à la Kaiser Wilhelm. To be fair to him he was obviously a good soldier with lots of very sensible ideas. The task given to him was that Perowne's Rifles, acting as infantry and sappers at the same time, were to man the bridges across the River Bethune which runs northwards from Forge-Les-Eaux, from Serqeux up towards Dieppe. Our actual zone of defence was as far as Neufchatel en Bray.

I can't remember quite how many bridges there were over what would now be considered a very small obstacle, the River Bethune, but it was a big enough obstacle to stop the tanks of the day. We were put in ordinary defensive positions along this river line with the bridges prepared for demolition. The only trouble was that we didn't have any modern weapons to speak of at all. We had a few

Boyes anti tank rifles, and we had a few Lewis guns, but no Bren guns. Otherwise we just had the ordinary Lee Enfield rifles which had been in army possession since before WW1. So we were unlikely ever to be a great obstacle to a fast moving German force, although of course we did not know that at the time.

The other thing we didn't have was any communications equipment whatsoever except possibly about five field telephones which had to be laid with wire to the three company headquarter positions on the River Bethune miles away. We had no radios of any sort.

During this time I was told to build a road block on the road outside our Battalion HQ which was in a lovely Norman barn 2 miles back from the river. Having been trained at Chatham what I did was to dig enormous great holes in the road and sink fairly powerful good sized tree stumps into them so that we had a zig-zag and more or less immovable road block which vehicles could just about get through. This was just around the corner from a bocage-like hedge.

Anyway, my friend, twin; soulmate and fellow schoolmate, Tony Poynder, was in the company based on Neufchatel en Bray. Being a lively character he had managed to find a Bugatti 25, a lovely French racing blue open sport's car. So he thought he would try it out. He came at the rate of knots along the French roads without taking too much care and hit my road block, boink, which was highly effective. It ruined the car. It threw him over the bocage hedge and he landed in an apple tree on the far side of the hedge piercing his lung and looking in no fit state to go on living. We managed to get an ambulance along fairly quickly, by some miracle, and we got him into the ambulance to send him off to the base hospital which was in Rouen, about 25 miles away. Apparently his language was so fluent under the anaesthetic and morphia in the ambulance that the doctor in command reckoned that he was worth saving, and indeed saved him. Nothing like a few old soldier stories!

Anyway, we didn't see much of the Germans. We had a few aircraft overhead and we did once or twice see reconnaissance units on motor bicycles coming towards our position, but we didn't have any fighting to do that I can recollect, while I was there anyway, so it wasn't a very active war for us at that stage. What we did see were thousands and thousands and thousands of refugees coming back through from the direction of Belgium and the French frontier areas, heading westwards as fast as they could go with all their baggage and everything else - back to safety somewhere. A most depressing sight. The Germans were having it all their own way with their Blitzkrieg and the French didn't seem to be doing anything whatsoever. It really was a very, very depressing state of affairs for newly joined soldiers and newly joined officers, for all of us in fact.

Some of these people hurrying back to safety as they saw it were, sadly, French soldiers who had discarded their arms and instead of having rifles slung over their shoulders they had slung loaves of bread. They had clearly no further wishes to face the enemy at all, not good for anybody's morale.

Well quite soon, and I am now talking about sometime towards the end of May, we were hearing more about the retreat towards Dunkirk I suppose.

We also heard that we were going to be relieved in the line by the 51st Highland Division and that the Perowne's Rifles, R.E., would come out of the line and head back in the general direction of the Bay of Biscay. We slowly packed up but not before the southern bit of our line near Serquex was attacked by Germans who came across the bridges over the River Bethune in French armoured cars with the correct recognition signals. When they got over the river in the cars which they had captured, with their guns reversed, they shot up the bridge demolition people. They captured the bridge intact, I believe, and I think that that is all that happened on the river Bethune at that southern end of the line.

Soon after this Col. Perowne left us and Perowne's Rifles came under the command of the second-in- command, Major Anstruther, under whose orders I really don't know. As a unit we went indeed towards the Bay of Biscay by truck and railway train and eventually landed up at a splendid hotel area called Pornichet which is south of La Baule. I suppose the evacuation of the British troops was at that time very much at the forefront in the minds of the planners, and that they possibly wanted to embark our lot at St. Nazaire on the ill fated Lancastria. I am very glad to say that that did not come to pass, otherwise we would all have been drowned – a greater loss of life than in H.M.S. Hood's subsequent sinking I believe.

Instead we had a thoroughly British solution and had a battalion parade of all things, with all formalities, on the local sport's ground, and we marched to the station, got into trains and instead of heading for St. Nazaire we headed for Cherbourg. We got there by train via Caen ahead of the Germans and I think the idea was to embark us as soon as possible in Cherbourg to get us back to England. As there was some time to spare and because we were engineers and had the ability, one or two detachments spent a happy time blowing up the cranes along the Cherbourg dockyard edges. Seeing a dockyard crane crashing twisted into the water is a very satisfactory sight if you have got that sort of mind.

Then eventually we were allotted a Belgian packet boat which was to take us back to England but the Belgian skipper refused to move out of Cherbourg inner harbour after we had embarked because he said there were parachute mines in the outer harbour and we would all get blown up. He was in a muck sweat of fright and our boss decided to pull his pistol out of his holster and poke it in this Belgian skipper's stomach and say "Get steaming mate, or else." So we steamed, and we had no less a ship doing anti aircraft protection out in the Channel at that time than H.M.S Hood. We didn't realise that at the time but that's a fact and we steamed from Cherbourg generally northwards to Southampton, arrived at Southampton docks, got off the boat and got into a train.

CHAPTER 3 – BACK IN ENGLAND

We were welcomed with hot sweet tea and buns by the WVS, who I don't think were Royal in those days, but they were extremely kind. We were all welcomed with waving flags as conquering heroes, although we hadn't conquered anything. We had at least got back with our arms intact and had not disgraced ourselves and indeed had had no opportunity so to do!

Exactly the date of all this I can't quite remember but it was well after Dunkirk had happened and so people were used to troops returning unexpectedly from France. Anyway we were put in a train at Southampton and our next stop was Hereford. We got out at Hereford and were marched to Hereford Race Course which was to be our home for the next week or so.

Hereford Race Course camp was commanded by a very fussy officer called Major Sebag Montefiore, who was I think in the 60th Rifles, and he didn't much like the look of us and we didn't really much like the look of him, so we were glad to stay there only for a week. We were really disbanded at Hereford Racecourse and never operated as a unit again or since. We went our ways back to various depots including Chatham, Kent.

There was one other unit I read about, or heard about, coming out of France at the same time. This was a gunner anti aircraft unit complete with all its guns which embarked themselves and their weapons at Brest and sailed from Brest, and arrived at Plymouth. On arrival at Plymouth their commanding officer lined them all up, congratulated them on having returned safely to England with all their weapons in good order. He then said, "You are now all members of a new club which has just been formed, life members indeed, and the name of the club is the Left Brest Club."

So much for those extraordinary days, I will now get on. The reason I landed up in 232 Field Company R.E. rather than anywhere else needs a little explaining. When we were at Chatham we were separately ordered to various units by the people there and my orders were to go North, half way up Scotland, to Elgin. My friend Bertie Baxter, who I was at school with earlier, had orders to join 232 Company at Weymouth. Well I'd spent a lot of my early life in the general area of Dorset and knew Weymouth and that coastline very well indeed and Bertie Baxter particularly wanted, for some other reason, no doubt an equally good one, to go to Elgin. So we agreed to change and the authorities couldn't have cared less who went to where.

On arrival with 232 I found that it was a Territorial Army Field Company R.E. in the 50th Northumbrian Division with its drill hall at Gateshead on the River Tyne in Northumberland. It was entirely populated by Geordies, all of whom were absolutely wonderful soldiers and wonderful craftsmen. But I couldn't understand a word they said, and they couldn't understand much about me either. After a week or two we got on together very well indeed and we were together in that unit from then, which was approximately July, 1940, until the unit finally got put in the bag by Rommel in the desert at the end of May, 1942. So by then we all knew each other pretty well.

232 Company was part of the 150th Infantry Brigade. The other units in the Brigade were the 4th East Yorks., the 4th and 5th Green Howards and the 72nd Field Regiment R.A. including 285 Battery, which played a particular part in the Desert War as far as I was concerned a year or more later. I will tell you about this in due course.

The task of 232 Field Company in the Weymouth area was to lay all the mines, supervise the construction of all pill boxes, prepare bridges for demolition and assist the Infantry in the preparation of field defences within the boundaries between Abbotsbury Swannery to the west and Anvil Point near Swanage to the east, which included the Chesil Bank, Portland Bill and Portland Island. (The wags in the R.N. ward rooms used to call Portland Bill "Willoughby Portland, Esq. R.N."!)

The most hideous and lethal mines were Royal Navy beach mines, which were extremely delicate and difficult to lay. Many got sucked away under their protective wire by the undertow of the ebbing tide on some of the beaches, beaches like Arishmel and Kimmeridge. We lost one officer and one sapper killed, and the Navy lost one rating killed during these operations.

Near the middle of September 1940, we were put on red alert as invasion was thought to be imminent. The task given to me and my section (platoon you might call it) was to man the road and railway bridges between Weymouth and Portland with my sappers. The Portland railway bridge no longer exists but the road bridge still does, and anyway, both these bridges were there then and were bounded on the Weymouth side by the Whitehead's torpedo works. We had already prepared them properly for demolition.

There were steel girders under the bridges and we had means of blowing them from either end of both bridges. If the enemy landed on Portland, I was to blow them and beat a retreat towards Weymouth. If they landed at Weymouth, vice versa. I'm not quite sure what would have happened if such an event had happened, but "them were the orders"!

In the mean time we had to keep the gun cotton, which was the demolition explosive, wet at all times because gun cotton has to be wet to achieve its full cutting force value. It is only the primers inside the wet gun cotton that need to be kept dry. So we spent a good deal of time keeping the gun cotton wet while we were waiting for the Germans to arrive. We had heard the code word "Cromwell" which was the warning order that they were coming, but they never came.

But what we did witness, beforehand and after, was much of the Battle of Britain being fought in daylight over the Dorset coast and this was really fascinating to watch in the lovely summer sunshine. Not funny seeing Spitfires or Hurricanes shot down obviously, but marvellous seeing a great many more Germans than Brits being shot down in these aerial battles.

When the flap started in September I drew three days rations for my 60 sappers, but we managed to eat all these in two days while the flap was on. As peacetime bureaucracy was still with us and later on when the auditors discovered that I'd eaten more rations than I should have done, or my soldiers had, I was ordered to pay for 60 rations out of the miserable 10/6 per day which was then my salary.

After we had completed all the work we had to do on the coast laying mines and preparing field defences and so on we had to move North a little bit and prepare another defence line in the general line of the River Frome between Dorchester and Wareham.

At this time we were working very near Cattistock, Dorset, which had been my home during many holidays when I was a boy and my parents were abroad on R.A.F. duty elsewhere. This was owned by the Atkinson family and the youngest son of the family was one of my great friends. That was Martin Atkinson, who later on got married and had a son called Robert who became my godson. Talking of godsons, the other half of this equation, Bertie Baxter, who went up to Elgin instead of coming down to Weymouth, as I have already explained, got married later and had a son called Peter. Many of you will have read or heard about Peter Baxter, who is the BBC Radio's cricket presenter for all the test matches around the world and elsewhere, and has been for many many years. He became my godson too, so as far as I was concerned I had two godsons who were intimately connected with the beginnings of WW2.

We were then moved, for no apparent reason, to North Somerset where the unit went to a place called Flax Bourton near Congesbury to the west of Bristol. The officers were billeted in Sir John and Lady Sinclair's country house at Flax Bourton in the greatest possible comfort; private squash court and all. We were very well looked after indeed, but hadn't been there long before the terrible bombing of Bristol started.

Because we were Sappers we were much in demand to help the Bristolians clear up all the mess caused by the bombing and pull down their damaged buildings, help with bomb disposal, deal with the water supply and generally do a grand job around Bristol. It was very, very hard work, which the soldiers really took to with enormous good will and with great skill. One of the more terrifying moments during that period was helping to get the George's Bristol Brewery dray horses, which were huge great percheron sized beasts, out of their bombed stables. As they went kind of spare as the bombing went on getting these huge animals out to safety before the stables went on fire was really a most hideous and frightening task.

Another less dangerous but nevertheless extremely memorable task was getting a bomb out of Harvey's wine cellars. A bomb went straight through the wine cellars, the tasting room and underground. After a bit of time we managed, with the help of trained bomb disposers, to get the bomb out safely, take it down to the beaches near Avonmouth, and blow the damn thing up. Harveys were naturally very grateful for this and made the Sappers more or less freemen of their cellars. So, if you could imagine 60 or 70 Geordies as freemen of the Harvey's Bristol cellars, you can imagine the subsequent hangovers and chaos that resulted. The recognised conducted tour started down at the Fino sherries at one end of the cellars and you went with your tasting glasses along the various barrels all the way through the Amontillados through to the Olorosos through to the Bristol Creams at the sweeter and strongest end and by the time you had completed even a part of this circuit you were completely stoned.

Two or three weeks after we had done our stuff, or as much as we could clearing up Bristol, we were moved to Burnham on Sea. Burnham on Mud would be a better name. This was as part of a general deployment of 150 Brigade, and we had no idea why we had been sent there. We subsequently did a military exercise, which in later days we discovered had some bearing on where we were to go next.

CHAPTER 4 – LIVERPOOL TO AFRICA

If you have drunk sufficient of Harvey's sherry and you have a map in front of you, you will immediately notice that the coast line of Somerset and North Devon, roughly between Westonsupermare and Barnstaple in Devon is the same shape as the part of Cyrenaica in North Africa between Tobruk and roughly Adjedabia. If you can imagine that Bridgewater is Tobruk then Minehead will be Derna. Dunkerry Beacon will be the top of the Jebel Akhdar or the Green Mountains. Lynton, Lynmouth will be roughly Cyrene. Ilfracombe will be roughly Benghazi, and Barnstaple, Devon would be roughly Adjedabia. So if you decided in your military wisdom, having sobered up a bit, to carry out an exercise there, you would be rehearsing the sort of thing that went on in the desert around about that time, and indeed later, where the opposing armies, the Allies against the German and Italian Afrika Corps under Rommel, would go to and fro across North Africa, fighting each other and then retreating and then going back the other way and so on.

So we did this once, and then went back to our billets in Burnham on Mud to find that of all things, we were being issued with some helmets, topees, solar topees. Immediately we were issued with solar topees, we knew that our next posting would be to Iceland or Russia or somewhere similar, certainly nowhere where topees were required. So we marched to the station in Burnham on Mud, or it may have been Highbridge. We got onto trains, and we got out of the trains in Liverpool, Merseyside and got into a Canadian Pacific liner called the Empress of Asia, where we met a number of our other friends in 150 Infantry Brigade, like Green Howards and East Yorks.

We set sail from the Mersey, we knew not in what direction, but started off by heading roughly North, to find ourselves in the Clyde picking up a few other ships, and then off again generally westward, with a touch of northing in it perhaps.

Still not knowing where the hell we were going we went on west and west and west, and we picked up more and more ships and we were escorted by a bigger and bigger naval force. I can't tell you how many naval ships there were, but there must have been over 20 in the escort. Eventually after a good deal of sailing generally westwards, we turned left and started sailing southwards. Presumably we were on the far side of Ireland by then, and heading generally towards the south.

We lived at pretty close quarters, officers probably in bunks about 10 to a cabin and of course the soldiers in hammocks down on the mess decks at 14" spacing in true naval fashion. The ship had its regular peacetime crew on boards, Lascars and Chinese, mostly Chinese, I suppose, from the Canadian Pacific side. The food was excellent and there was plenty to drink, in the officer's mess area anyway. There were Chinese stewards, and you would order a round for you and your friends of 3 beers, 2 gin and limes, 3 whiskys and soda, and 2 of this and 4 of that, and the steward would come along with his tray and say,

"Here it is, Mister, three shillings and sixpence!"

We spent our days doing various sorts of training, giving lectures, taking a lot of exercise on deck, playing games, boxing matches, that sort of thing, anyway trying to keep as fit as possible. We did a certain amount of reading, quite apart from our exercising ourselves in the bars. After about a week of all this the convoy seemed to speed up a bit and we lost sight of a whole lot of ships which went more or less eastwards instead of going on southwards. Presumably these were going through on a Mediterranean convoy although we didn't know of course what was happening in any detail at all. But we went on south with slightly increased speed and with a much smaller naval escort.

All I particularly remember about that bit of the voyage was that I got a violent dental pain which was an impacted wisdom tooth, which the ship's doctor people could do nothing about. They had no anaesthetic and no means of heaving this damn tooth out. So I went on in considerable pain and was eventually allowed ashore when we stopped to take on coal at Freetown in Sierra Leone. Indeed the only two officers allowed ashore at Freetown, S.L, was the commanding General, and 2nd Lt., I think I might have been a Lieutenant by then, John Cowtan, to have his wisdom tooth dealt with.

I went ashore there, went up to the RAMC barracks and little hospital above Freetown and they said that they would be delighted to get my tooth out but they very much regretted that they hadn't got any anaesthetic either. But they said I needn't worry and took me along to their officer's mess where they pulled a little curtain back from a picture rail. I wasn't quite sure what I was going to see underneath, whether maybe it was something that the butler had seen, but it wasn't that at all. It was a recipe for snakebite which was an anaesthetic invented in their officer's mess, 2 or 3 drams of which would knock anybody out. So they duly knocked me out and they removed my wisdom tooth. I don't remember very much about it except seeing just before I finally passed out a thing that looked just like a penny farthing bicycle which turned out to be a dentist's drill driven by a foot pedal. I don't really remember very much else because the snakebite had taken full effect and I woke up in a hospital bed, I suppose it was the next morning, with a grinning black West African bringing me hot sweet tea in an enamel mug. So I swallowed that gratefully and although I still had a slight pain in the face got back to the ship and related all my experiences and that is the only time I have ever set foot in Sierra Leone I'm glad to say. I don't wish to go back there at all but it was great having a day on shore even under those circumstances.

Having got all the new coal on board, the stoking crew, who were Liverpool Irish for some reason, decided to go on strike. The Captain of the vessel, being a properly brought up sailor, threw them in the brig and clapped them in irons where they remained until we made an emergency stop in Capetown to take on a Cape Coloured stoking crew. The stoking of the ship's boilers was done on the way down by a detachment of the Dirty Durham Light Infantry who were all miners and who all understood about shovels and coal and could not have been a better bunch of stokers. So we went right down Africa and arrived in a brilliantly lit Capetown – no blackout down there at that time anyway.

Continuing on from Capetown we went through the Roaring 40's in very rough seas indeed to Durban. We hadn't actually refuelled in

Capetown. We had just taken on the Cape Coloured stoking crew. We had a planned stop in Durban for a week for recoaling for the final bit of the voyage up to Suez and Egypt. Durban was brightly lit and there was a huge crowd of very welcoming South Africans. We all went ashore, officers, soldiers, the whole lot and we continued going ashore in batches for the whole week. We weren't allowed to pay for anything at all. Everything was on the house and we had a simply marvellous time as you can imagine, going to bars and restaurants and dance halls and all sorts in the town and also going out into the country a bit to places like the Country Club and the Zoo.

We steamed on north without any more stopping, crossing the Equator for the second time and arriving at the South end of the Red Sea. Then up the Red Sea where it was getting hotter and hotter and hotter, until we arrived at Port Tewfik at the southern end of the Suez Canal and dropped anchor. Still smouldering in the harbour was the liner, I think it was called Georgic, that somehow had got bombed by the Germans, when it was stationary in Port Tewfik. Anyway, it wasn't a very pleasant sight.

The first thing that all new military arrivals had to do was to get acclimatised to the local conditions, and so in true tradition we slung our topees into the drink and we got into the train at Port Tewfik, Suez, and we detrained at a place in the desert between Ismailia and Tel el Kebir called Quassasin, which was to be our home for the next 10 days or fortnight, while we got our knees brown.

The next move of the unit was operational and we had to move to somewhere just to the East of Mersa Matruh on the coast of the Western Desert of Egypt to come under the temporary command of the 4th Indian Division, until the rest of the Brigade and indeed the rest of the 50th Division joined up.

I was despatched with all our drivers to Port Said where I was to pick up the vehicles that we had loaded at Liverpool as they came off the ship. They had been in one of the ships in the big convoy and had got to Port Said obviously through the Mediterranean rather than round the bottom. All the vehicles were there. They were intact and we drove them southwards to Kantara and Ismailia and then to Cairo where we had to have a certain amount of maintenance and replacement of this and that done at the Base Vehicle Depot at Bbassia. I had the lucky opportunity of being able to get the day off to go and visit the flat on Qezira Island where my family had lived for a year or two when my father was the principal RAF medical officer, Middle East, and where I had been to before on holidays from Wellington College. The same doorman or boab was asleep as usual at the front door, but on being woken up he seemed to be quite glad to see me again!

After some excellent hospitality, I had reluctantly to return to the unit, and we got into the vehicles and drove them via the Pyramids all the way to Alexandria. We then turned left and drove them slowly in good order to find the unit near Mersa Matruh, stopping I think it was at Kilo80, I can't quite remember, Sidi Hanif, or somewhere roughly of that name, where you could still buy beer at the NAAFI. It was the last place you <u>could</u> buy beer before going on a ration of 2 cans a week for the forseeable future.

The unit seemed glad to see me back, or anyway they were very glad to get their own vehicles back and I think rather surprised that the whole lot were there without any damage to any of them, so I felt quite good about that.

We then got on with our job which was under the control of the C.R.E of the 4th Indian Division. We were to lay minefields on both sides of the main road and up on top of the escarpment against a return visit from the Axis forces heading towards Alexandria. This they did not actually do for some time to come. So it was mines, mines, mines and mines. That was the story of our life in the desert for a long time to come; except for a happy gap in Cyprus in the middle, which I will come to in due course.

There was a Polish Brigade also under the command of the 4th Indian Division immediately to our East and the Polish engineer company was just the other side of a minefield 300 yards from us. They, very hospitably, invited two of us to have supper with them one evening, which involved going through the minefield to get to them. Of course we had cleared minefield gaps so that transport could go through, and these were twisty gaps so that if there were vehicles coming through them, and possibly enemy air attacks coming, it meant that enemy aircraft couldn't go absolutely straight down a gap to shoot up vehicles going through it because the vehicles were going through in a zig zag manner. Anyway, Roger Vasey, a fellow troop commander and I went to sup with the Poles. We were wined and dined rather more heavily than we had expected and drank the most enormous quantities of Polish vodka of one sort or another and were really in no fit state at all to carry on the war for a bit.

We were in Roger's vehicle and the Poles, in their hospitable manner, had sent out two or three sappers of their own, unknown to us, to straighten out the gap through the minefield so that we would have a straight journey home instead of having to weave through the zig zags. Of course when you start pulling the salients out of a twisty minefield gap you expose the mines which were previously held in by some of the twists. Sure enough we struck one with an almighty bang and it did the vehicle no good and it did neither of us any good either. I must say that when eventually we were heaved out and so to speak pulled ashore back into our own lines our commanding officer wasn't best pleased. The vehicle was a write off, Roger Vasey was intact, and I was more or less intact except that I received the only wound that I was to get during the whole of WW2. This was a bit of something going into my right arm which hurt a bit but did no further damage and was cured very easily by our own doctor in a week or two. Our C.O. was very good and we heard no more about it at all, nor did we repeat the process of visiting our friends the Poles who were duly amused I think by the whole event in a somewhat Slavic sort of way.

While all this was going on the Germans were invading Crete. The Battle of Crete of course has been written about and told on many occasions. In fact it was a battle which was led by the German Airborne Forces who did a magnificent job with great bravery but were so damaged that they were never used as a full airborne formation again during the whole of WW2.

CHAPTER 5 – CYPRUS

After a while, we were whipped in a hurry out of our position near Mersa Matruh and put into trucks and driven to Alexandria where we embarked in the cruiser H.M.S Neptune, as a whole unit complete with our vehicles. We travelled by night we knew not where, but discovered that we were heading for Cyprus. We proceeded at the rate of knots, and I mean somewhere about 35 knots, I believe, to the east end of Cyprus, where the port of Famagusta lies. The depth of water at Famagusta was insufficient for H.M.S Neptune to go alongside so we had to transship several miles to the east into Destroyers that had come to meet us. We were taken into Famagusta and debarked from them in the early morning of some day I suppose in June/July, 1941 and we started to do our task of putting Cyprus into a state of defence.

Our unit was moved to a bit of Cyprus near Larnaca. It was between the town of Larnaca and the salt pans, and our main task to start off with was to try and put in obstacles to German airborne glider landings on flat areas roundabout. At the same time the C.R.E of 50th Division called Jonah Kennedy*, who arrived fairly soon afterwards, organised large quantities of Cypriot labour to build pillboxes and defensive positions on these possible landing grounds. So the local sappers such as us had also to look after bunches of enforced Cypriot labour in the preparation of these concrete obstacles and pillboxes. That was quite a hard task in the heat and dust of the place.

(The C.R.E's son much later on became an Airborne Sapper Officer in what is now 9 Para Squadron R.E., and was killed mine-lifting in Palestine in 1945 when I was O.C. of that unit.)

There was an enormous shortage of water and although the British had been running the administration of Cyprus for some years, they had in no way expected the arrival of a complete division of between 10 and 20,000 British soldiers for defensive purposes at any time. As well as a shortage of water there was also a shortage of food, and generally speaking one lived on fairly short rations.

However the Commander of the Royal Army Service Corps of 50th Division, whose name I cannot recollect, was an ingenious fellow. Knowing about the shortage of food, particularly of meat, he organised the purchase of large numbers of beef animals, calves and the like, from the Lebanon to be shipped to Cyprus as soon as possible.

We in 232 Field Company were given the task of making arrangements for these beef cattle to be met at the Port of Larnaca which was a shallow water place, unshipped into rafts, and driven ashore. This was no easy task as you can imagine. The way we solved it was by requisitioning local barges and building platforms on them, getting quantities of canvas and making shutes so that the cattle coming from the Lebanon could be hog tied and turned upside down on the shutes and slid down on their backs to the waiting platforms on the requisitioned barges, then taken ashore. Our experiences, I think, in getting the dray horses out of the George's Brewery in Bristol, which I have mentioned earlier in these recollections, stood us in good stead when unloading lively Lebanese cattle from the platforms on these temporary rafts that we had constructed.

Another task that the company was given, and it was handed by the commanding officer to me, was to start the construction of a base hospital at Dhakelia. This was just a blank patch on the map at that time, now of course it is a built up area. Then it was just a field used for sheep. It had a very small bay with a little building on it, which was a port control decontamination area for unwanted visitors to Cyprus; a quarantine station you might call it. Anyway, there we were, and I was told to build a base hospital which of course was not made of concrete or anything like that, but would have been a hutted camp. So we decided roughly what we wanted. Of course the thing needed surveying, and because my RE training had been cut short earlier in the war, as I think I have described - by the urgency of the requirement for sending troops to France - I had missed my survey course. Although I had been issued with some very good survey tools like proper theodolites and so on I had to admit that I really had not the slightest idea of how to use them.

So I fell in my soldiers as usual and explained the situation, and asked if there was anybody there who was thoroughly familiar with the use of these tools, because we had to build a hospital, and the sooner the hospital was finished the sooner the beautiful nurses would arrive, and everybody would be that much happier. Whereupon one soldier leapt to attention, a corporal, and I said,

"Yes, what is it, Corporal Longbottom?"

"Well, Sir, I was the Borough Surveyor of Blythe, and I do know how to use those things."

So happily I told Corporal Longbottom that from here on in he was in charge of the entire operation and to kindly get on with it with all possible speed.

And then I suppose the biter was bitten, because I went down with a bad attack of dysentery which needed curing in what was the base hospital, then a bunch of tents in an olive grove not too far away from Dhakelia. They put the right sort of medicine into me and sent me off for a short recovery course up the mountains of Troodos to the Berengaria Hotel at Platres which was totally painless. After a week or so there, where I ended up drinking a great deal of local vino and learning how to play bridge (of all things at that time!) I returned to the unit, to Corporal Longbottom and the rest. There I found that the new base hospital had been laid out and that the arrangements had been put in place for starting to bring in stores to build the huts on the places that had been chosen.

At which stage I was ordered by my commanding officer and the C.R.E to do a useful job for once and to carry out a demolition reconnaissance of the entire island of Cyprus against the possible arrival of the Germans, who I am glad to say had not arrived at that stage. I was to get on with this with all possible speed and report on what demolitions were required and roughly how they should be carried out.

After considerable thought about this and obvious discussion with my boss and the colonel, it was decided that so far as the port demolitions were concerned Famagusta was the most important port and should be priority one. Second priority port was Limasol, and third but low priority was Kyrenia, the port in the North of Cyprus. The next main task would be the railway line. It was a sort of Micky Mouse meter gage railway line that ran from Famagusta all the way across the plain to Nicosia and on from Nicosia to Murphou and the copper mines at a place called Skouriotissa. It was considered important to demolish the bridges on this railway line, make the thing inoperable should anybody want to use it and at the same time make sure that the operations at the copper mine at Skouriotissa should be capable of being put on hold pretty quickly, as apparently this was an important military objective, or so it was considered at the time. Finally, and I didn't quite understand at the time, and still don't, I was to reconnoitre the possibility of laying mines across the narrow part of the Karpas Peninsula (the "Parr Handle") which is in the North East of the island. I suppose that it was wanted to have a barrier in between the main part of the island and a place of possible withdrawal from the island. Don't ask me why.

By that time I had acquired a very nice Humber pickup vehicle which held three of us comfortably with our kit and measuring devices. The reconnaissance party for this great task consisted of Lance Sergeant Lionel Longbottom, whom I had promoted from Corporal to Lance Sergeant, because I was taking all the credit for all the good work he had done on the new base hospital at Dhakelia, and Driver Foster. So we packed all our kit into this vehicle and we took off. I more or less had permission to go anywhere I liked in Cyprus, to stop at any village I wanted to and to get the local Muktar, or headman, to give us accommodation and bring us food and water, wine or whatever, and just to get on with it. So this is what we did.

We did it in the order of priority just mentioned and it was the most enormously interesting job and the greatest possible fun. There were of course many great moments, and there simply isn't space to record all of these, but I do recall arriving eventually at the copper mines at Skouriotissa to find that they were run by an American mining company, who were good hospitable people. When we got there we were taken to their mess room and then to the bar and they said, "Lieutenant, what is your poison?" I said my poison was scotch whisky and they asked the others what they wanted to drink. Instead of just giving each of us a glass of whatever we wanted, they gave each of us a bottle of what we had asked for, which was real hospitality and the end of a very good part of that particular reconnaissance of the Cyprus railroad. *

Later, having finally completed my task by having done the recce of this extraordinary minefield across the Karpas Peninsula, I got back to our HQ and reported on the demolition recce. Very soon after that we were told that we were going to pack up and go somewhere else. In the mean time the rest of the 50th Northumbrian Division had arrived in the island of Cyprus and my story in Cyprus stops there and goes on to the next phase.

* I returned to Skouriotissa by parachute some 20 odd years later as an umpire on a 44 Parachute Brigade exercise.

CHAPTER 6 - PALESTINE

The next phase was being ordered back to the Port of Famagusta, where we embarked, not this time in H.M Destroyers, but at dead of night in a fast Minelayer called H.M.S Abdiel. We all got into this Minelayer, and we travelled by night at enormous speed, 40 knots I believe. We woke up the next morning to find that we were in Haifa in Palestine. Without anybody telling us the why and the wherefore of this rather sudden move, having arrived in Haifa, we were again put into vehicles and 232 Field Company was moved northwards on the Acra road to a place called Jammla on the Brook Kishon of biblical fame, which is where the roads to Nazareth and Nablus fork. We went into a tented camp at Jermana.

The Brook Kishon was narrow and slow moving with excellent cover on both banks, and it was teeming with game. I had my trusty 16 bore with me and shot several species of duck, two species of snipe, two of partridge and a woodcock, of all things!

After we had been there for a bit and still not really knowing what we were at, the Brigade H.Q. arrived including the Brigade Commander, Brigadier Bill Haydon, who had been our Brigade Commander all along. This very stern, soldierly character of the Middlesex Regiment, (the Diehards), was very stiff on discipline and very keen on everyone being soldierly, smart and very fit at all times. We even had to polish the ammunition which we kept in our holsters to fill our pistols 38, and furthermore he expected us to run up to the top of Mount Carmel every morning which was one hell of a task, and very much more than in the previous months when we had been in the North Somerset area. There we had had to run up to the top of Brent Knoll, which we had considered quite hard work then. But Brent Knoll and Mount Carmel do not compare in height!

I was able thankfully to get my gun out at times and go along the Brook Kishon and shoot snipe, woodcock, the odd pigeon, an occasional partridge and so on. I think practically everything was out of season, but that didn't really fuss me too much. It was coming on September by then so perhaps it was all alright. I did shoot the odd duck as well, so that was the greatest possible fun. Sadly we were so badly paid in those days that we didn't have enough money to attend any of the bright lights of Haifa, but life wasn't too bad otherwise. We were able to entertain the soldiers as best we could with the means at our disposal. We got hold of a contractor and set up cinema films in our camp and things of that sort.

Looking back on it, it was amazing that nobody told us why we were really there. It was a long time afterwards that I discovered that the main reason we had been moved to Palestine was not, as some people supposed, to help in the subsequent operations against the Vichy French, who had been so much of a problem in Syria and Lebanon, but because we were going up to the Caucasus of all places somewhere beyond Rostock on Don to prepare a defence line against the Germans coming south from Russia into the Middle East. We knew nothing of that at the time I'm glad to say.

CHAPTER 7 – LIFE IN THE DESERT

Anyway, instead of that we were ordered back to Egypt and by one means or another we went down through Palestine. We crossed Sinai. We crossed over the Suez Canal once again. We got into vehicles once again, and we drove back all the way to the Mersa Matruh area and on beyond it towards the Egyptian Cyrenaican/ Libyan frontier, Sidi Barani, or somewhere up there.

It must have been roundabout Christmas I recall, but at about that time I was riding a motor bike for some extraordinary reason. It was a Harley Davidson which was issued in lieu of B.S.A's which they seemed to have run out of. I was urgently requiring to do my morning devotions during a very severe sandstorm, and I bared my bottom and sat down. Unfortunately because of the sand storm I hadn't realised that I was sitting on a pile of camel thorn, so that was not a particularly successful morning.

Talking of sandstorms seems a good moment to explain a bit about desert life and carrying on day to day in the conditions that existed. The sand storms themselves would be blown up from the south by the winds called Hamsins and they'd last for about three days, just went on and on and on and everything was covered. You couldn't see in front of you. Your eyes were full of muck and sand. Your ears were full. Your mouth was full. It got in everywhere, under your clothes, into your food, into your water supply, through your anti gas goggles which you wore against sand storms and into your mouth. It got onto the vehicles, and the beating of sand against the metal of the vehicles caused tremendous storage of static electricity. Sometimes you would go up to touch one of the vehicles and you'd have a huge electric spark of static electricity firing across between the vehicles and yourself. Those sand storms were one of the most horrible things to have to live with in desert conditions. The only really good thing about them was that it was just as bad for the enemy as it was for yourself.

Now I'd like to comment on water. The normal supply of water, certainly when we were in static conditions in the Gazala Line and north of Tobruk, came from brackish wells with water very heavily chlorinated. It wasn't until much later when well-boring units arrived and discovered artesian wells under the second ridge up the desert that we ever got any decent tasting or constant water supply. Anyway the ration of water was at the best one gallon per head per day. The order of priority was to fill your personal water bottle daily, then to top up the vehicle radiators of your unit daily so that they were always ready for use. Then you had to issue 3 pints of water per day approximately to the cooks for them to use for hydrating dehydrated vegetables, for supplying up to three mugs of tea per head per day and for any other cooking jobs that they had. The balance of the water was pooled, as far as we were concerned, in sections of 10 people. So after you have done all the things I have just mentioned you had a bit of water left and you put it all together amongst 10 people. You had to shave every day, and when you'd shaved, you filtered the water through a sort of sand and colander filter, and it went back to be shared amongst the rest. Then you each washed as best you could, particularly in the relevant places, like under the armpits, in the crutch, up your arse and in between your toes. Then you filtered all that again, which made another nasty mess. About once every ten days the balance of water on any one day was given to one of the ten in the section to do with whatever he liked. Well there wasn't very much left, of course, maybe a pint or two at the very most. So some people just liked to stand there stark naked and have it poured over them. So water supply, and the way it was handled, was not funny and many people simply would not believe what one had to go through because of the lack of it.

As far as sleeping was concerned we all had to dig our own slit trenches which had the dual purpose of providing somewhere to live and somewhere to fight and to observe from. Everyone was supplied with a bivouac tent. You had to dig your trench so that you could use your bivouac tent as part of your living and fighting accommodation.

As far as latrines were concerned, you dug deep latrines like Lem put it, "dig 'em wide and dig 'em deep", but of course you had to get to them, and in sand storms it wasn't all that easy. If there were severe sandstorms you laid minefield guidance tape from where you slept to where you shat, so that you didn't get lost either on the way there, or more particularly on the way back. This again is difficult to believe but very true indeed.

As far as food was concerned of course one got a daily ration which got a bit monotonous because it was bully and then again bully and then bully again and a biscuit to go with the bully; and then more biscuit and more biscuit. Sometimes you got tinned pilchards which were pretty disgusting but better than continuous bully until you got some more tinned pilchards when you'd rather have bully again. And then you had indescribably indigestible sausages; tinned sausages. Where they were made and who made their fortune illegally by supplying them I simply do not know, but they were absolutely disgusting. Occasionally, and that was on high days and very much holidays, one got a tin of fruit and of course the real mecca of a tin of fruit would be a tin of peaches in their juice, because it not only provided sweetness, but it provided liquid. Tinned peaches were pearls beyond price if you like to put it that way.

We got a ration of cigarettes. Originally we got a round tin of 50 Players cigarettes per week, and they were lovely to have and always much in demand. But of course they ran out and the only cigarettes that appeared after the Players ran out were Victory V's made, I think, in the North of India or some desert up in I don't know where. I think they were made of what the camels and goats left and so on, all crushed up and dried and then rolled up in paper and put in a fancy box called Victory V. I didn't bother to smoke mine, after the first one, so I kept most of them for some of the soldiers who were cigaretteoholics, so to speak. I thought rather they have them than me throw them away, but they were really disgusting.

And then of course we had our two cans of beer per week. Now that was really all right indeed, but that was it. After you'd passed Kilo40, or was it 80, on the road between El Alamein and Sidi Barani, you were on 2 cans a week.

The other thing that came up with the rations was lemonade powder which you could mix with any water you happened to have over from your own personal ration in addition to your two cans of beer, but you didn't get any extra water ration to mix with it. So, there we were. That was the food. The cooks did marvels with what they had. They had various recipes for making bully not taste like bully, but to taste more like bully after you'd digested it and so on. So there were dehydrated vegetables, the odd pilchard, the odd lemonade, and the very, very occasional Victory V smoke and 2 cans of beer per week. What a life!

You might also wonder about travel. Well, we being sappers, were wheel borne. We didn't have to march very far anywhere thank God. We always went in vehicles. That meant you had to have maps which weren't particularly good. Certainly you couldn't operate on what soldiers have nowadays which is called a Global Positioning System, which means that you always know where you are at any one time. Well, we had to think that we always knew where we were at any one time and be able by some means or another to get to the next point where we thought we wanted to go. You did it by very careful measurement from where you thought you were and where you thought you wanted to go. You had to get the distance, then the bearing, which you worked out with a protractor and then you put that bearing on a prismatic compass or onto a sun compass. You travelled along using your prismatic compass and your sun compass and/or by day or by night using your speedometer measurements for measuring the distance between where you were and where you thought you wanted to go.

Sometimes at night you went quite long distances using the stars as basic bearing points, and as long as you didn't travel on the same star for more than 20 minutes you could carry out some pretty accurate navigation that way. Of course you used the sun which went the usual way round in the desert, like it does anywhere else, when you could, and of course you got stuck every now and again in some bits of the desert. Some parts were very hard and some parts weren't, and you had to be ready to get stuck in sand or similar. So you had to carry sand tracks with you and know how to use them and know how to drive across soft sand without bogging yourself in. Of course every time you used the vehicles you had to go through the old business of WOFLTB, which means checking the water, the oil, the fuel, the lights, the tyres and the batteries. Good old WOFLTB, it has saved many a life; never to be forgotten. We called it "Waffle TB"

Of course all these problems of daily life became routine and one didn't think about them so much, but one jolly well had to learn them. Anyone arriving newly to your unit as a reinforcement had to learn these things pretty quickly or he would not easily survive, or alternatively he wouldn't be very easy to live with until he had learnt them.

CHAPTER 8 – GAZALA LINE

At this stage of the war and I'm talking about mid January, 1942, the state of affairs in the desert was that the Axis Forces under General Rommel were back towards the west in the area on the far side of the Jebel Akhdar on the Libyan/Cyrenaic border south of Agedabia. We, the Allies, were in Tobruk and northwards. The line called the Gazala line was being formed. Gazala was a desert spot on the coast to the west side of Tobruk, and the Gazala line was a line of fortified positions covered by mines mostly running northwards from Gazala up as far as an old desert fort called Bir Hacheim some 35 miles away.

The part nearest the sea up to the top of the escarpment was held by a South African Division. Then from the escarpment going southwards towards Bir Hacheim came the 50th Infantry Division which was in 3 Brigades, 151 Brigade, 69 Brigade and ourselves, 150 Brigade, Gott-el-Ualeb. There was a huge gap in between 69 Brigade and 150 Brigade, our Brigade, a gap of I suppose 15 miles, which was not covered by any infantry at all. This was first of all because there weren't enough infantry to go around. Secondly because whoever was the commanding General, 8th Army, of the time, I think it was Auchinleck, decided that the centre part could be covered by the main reserves of an armoured brigade and a half coming up into the line if required. I may have got that wrong but I wasn't the commanding General.

To start off with 150 Brigade were put at the top of the escarpment next to the South Africans, and as the others came up they moved to the South of us. We eventually were taken out of the first position we were in by another South African Brigade. We were moved to

Gott-el Ualeb where this part of the Desert War stopped as far as 150 Brigade was concerned, as I shall explain later.

I am now talking about the time in roughly January, February of 1942 after we had come from Cyprus and we had crossed over into Cyrenaica. At that time the Germans had withdrawn and their line of defence was roughly from Tmimi and Derna on the sea near the Jebel Akhdar all the way round via Melhil to Benghazi, Agedabia and generally to the west. There was really a No man's land of anything up to 80 miles in between us in the 8th Army, and the German's Afrika Korps.

The way that the War went was that the British orders were to keep operating in the huge gap in between us and the Germans to try and dominate no man's land and prevent the Germans coming out of their positions further to the west. The way that this domination was carried out was by sending out battalion group columns, all motorised, to go and do specific jobs against the Germans in different places. A battalion column going out would consist of a whole battalion of infantry, possibly two, certainly one, battery of 25 pounder guns and a battery of 20mm Bofors guns, a battery of 2 pounder anti tank guns on portees and a certain amount of armoured car cover out in front. The armoured car cover was provided by South African and British Cavalry Regiments, like the 12th Lancers.

In the meantime each Brigade in the line was responsible for its own protection, laying minefields all round itself as far as possible. Of course there was the problem of the huge gap where there was no infantry and no defences, and these had to be filled. It was filled by laying two enormous minefields. One was called Hackney Marsh and one was called Stepney Marsh. Mine marshes they became and they were apparently very formidable objects, but they weren't quite as formidable as they should have been because we didn't have enough Infantry or Gunners to cover them and a minefield is not really very much good unless it is covered by fire. The enemy can get into it and be got out of it if it is covered by fire, or be driven out of it, or shot out of it if you like, but if there is nothing for them to shoot at, once they have got round the actual mines that have blown up or got through the mines that haven't been blown up there is nothing to stop them coming right on through, and this is exactly what happened later.

To understand the size of the problem you have to do a little simple mathematics. If one mile is approximately 2000 yards, then the length of the Gazala Line was approximately 35 miles, so we are talking about 70,000 mines, laid at 1 mine per yard of front, and that is if they were laid in a straight line from one end to the other. Then you must remember that you have got to lay mines around the back of you as well as just along the front, not all the way perhaps because sometimes you can get around doing that by putting in dummy minefields. You had to mark the minefields anyway with wire each side and with minefield signs on them, triangles hanging off the wire, but you didn't have to tell anybody that the mine was dummy or not or that the minefield was dummy. This was part of the deception here and there.

But suffice it to say that far from there being just 70,000 mines laid on the Gazala line which was the requirement of one mine per yard of front, in fact there were more like 350,000 mines laid altogether, because the mine marshes were laid thick, sometimes as much as 10 mines per yard of front to prevent enemy getting through in one fell swoop so to speak.

It was a very formidable task, and it was almost entirely carried out by the Sappers. They had to mark all the mines on maps so that they could subsequently be lifted, and indeed we needed mine maps so that if we had to go through them ourselves, (as we had to in a small way which I will explain later), then we knew where they were and how to get through them without damaging ourselves. All the Sappers had to become properly trained in how to handle these mines and they had to be trained in how to lay them properly and in an effective fashion. We had to become really mine conscious and not get careless in any way at all, and indeed we had no casualties through people being stupid or not obeying the rules in laying these minefields. This does great credit to all the Sappers themselves in my opinion.

To keep people's brains working properly and to provide a little light relief during these very hard-working days I decided to initiate a competition to design the best sort of anti-personnel mine. This was won by a certain Sapper, a Geordie, for designing an anti Italian psychological anti personnel mine. What would happen was that some unsuspecting Italian soldier would be stepping over the wire in the front of a minefield in some advance or another, and there would be a little bang go off underneath his foot, and being an Italian, instead of pressing on he would leap backwards, he reckoned at least three metres, and the little bang underneath his feet would have started off a small charge which would blow up in the time it took for him to leap back approximately three metres, so when he arrived 3 metres back he would then be blown up by a very much bigger charge and the whole thing would be very nasty indeed. *"Whey yon booger..."*

It was from our first position on the escarpment on the Gazala Line that we were to go out on one of our battalion group aggressive patrols. At this time, about early March, 1942, the situation in Malta was getting particularly critical through lack of supplies, ammunition etc. and it was quite essential for the Royal Navy to be able to escort ships through the Mediterranean from the Gibraltar end, to get them to reinforce Malta with supplies, material ammunition of all sorts and fuel. So it was decided by the Commanders in Chief that there would be several columns going out from the Allied lines, the Gazala line, and elsewhere, to as near the Mediterranean coast as possible, which was occupied by the Germans and the Italians, and to blow up as many aircraft as they could from the ground. This was also to encourage the enemy air forces, both Italian and German, to come and shoot at us on the ground instead of being available to shoot up the convoys that were planned to go into Malta to reinforce the place.

Anyway my section of Sappers, became part of a 4th East Yorks Battalion group to head out to a place called Martuba Airfield, which was 70 miles behind the lines, 70 miles through No-man's Land. We were to get into a position to shoot up the aircraft that were there on the airfield. We didn't in those days have anything like helicopters for observation. We didn't even have any light aircraft available for the same purpose, so observation of artillery fire had to be done by eye from the ground. A preliminary measurement of the topography round Martuba airfield indicated that there was nowhere sufficiently high for the gunners to be able to see where their fall of shot was and whether it was properly damaging the aircraft which they were sent to shoot up. So a further very careful map survey was done by the Survey Sappers and they found a spot which we could just about get to within Gunner range of Martuba Airfield. The range of a 25 pounder was really at the maximum about 12,000 yards, but you needed to get a bit closer than that in order to see the fall of shot.

We needed to build an observation tower for the Gunner observation people to climb up and from which they would be able to see. In the event this involved building a tower, 35 ft. high, which had to be carried from our position on the Gazala Line across 70 miles of desert and this desert included some very, very rough desert indeed; this was wilderness, rocky, very overgrown, nasty going desert. So it was given to us, as usual. The Sappers had to do everything like that, and we built a tower out of tubular scaffolding. We had a couple of platforms on it, first of all to strengthen it, and secondly eventually to stand on, and we put Jacob's ladders up the side. It was fairly stable when erected, but it was still extremely frightening trying to climb it, and anyway how the hell were we going to get it there?

Well what we did was make a special trellis work to fit on the back of what would now be called a 3 ton truck. We were able to tie this erection down complete on this trellis work on the back of the truck, and after a lot of practice the drivers could manoeuvre this affair across country in the most difficult conditions without the thing coming off. We set off to do this trip, and we drove through the day and through the night, and eventually got to the position required. The tower itself was designed by Major Harry Clapham, R.A., who was O.C. of 285th Battery of the 72nd Field Regiment, and myself, so we were both mutually dependent on each other to make sure that the thing worked.

We did get it to the place and we heaved it up into the vertical position, and we held it in position with guy ropes that we had taken with us so that the thing was relatively stable and there it was, the height of the platform being some 30 foot above ground level. Not very much fun really to have to climb up that – plain terrifying in fact! Both of us agreed that we were unlikely to be able to do so unless we had a sharpener to start with and fortunately I had a little rum left from some other event, so we had a good tot of rum each and we got Harry Clapham up to the top all right, and we got me up to the top with him.

I didn't stay up there. I came down again as quickly as possible and he was then able to start directing his artillery onto Martuba

Airfield. It was a very unpleasant set of orders that the Commanding Officer, Colonel Norman, had had. Harry Chapman had to stay in position from when he got there which was near enough dawn until 7.30p.m. which was near enough dark, because those were the times that the aeroplanes which were reputed to be on Martuba Airfield and elsewhere would be able to attack us, and we were to stay where we were, being attacked, regardless of what was shot up and what casualties there were until nightfall, so that those aeroplanes doing it could not also operate against the Malta convoy that was going through.

So there we sat in the greatest possible discomfort firing the guns until they were knocked out. We were then on the receiving end from the Allied axis airforces, the Luftwaffe and the Reggio Aeronautica, as sitting targets there for some 10 hours, something like that, and we were not allowed to move away. We had to stay there being targets. We had some casualties, which will hardly surprise you, but not nearly as many as one might have expected. We lost most of the guns and the gun teams were shot up and we lost the anti aircraft guns quite quickly. They were all shot up. The anti tank guns on Portees weren't any use anyway because there weren't any tanks to shoot up. None of them came out at us, and we didn't have to use our personal weapons except to fire our rifles and our Bren guns in a rather hopeless manner at these aircraft coming in at us. So one way and another we were extremely lucky through an extremely unpleasant operation.*

Somehow we got back to the Gazala Line. Because we had had a hairy time I put in for a special rum ration for my soldiers. This was a normal thing to do if you'd had a really tough time. You had to have an indent signed by a competent medical officer authorising the issue of rum and fortunately we had a competent medical officer who was our friend, who really was an incompetent medical officer in that instead of authorising the approved amount of 3/8 of a pint of rum per head he put it down as 3/8 of a gallon per head, so that is quite a lot of rum when you come to think of it, and it made up for a hell of a lot of hardship that we had had, and it made up for some more hardships that we were going to have for several weeks to come. We didn't obviously tell anybody that we had an incompetent medical officer, but what fun that was. Very good for morale.
Dad won an MC for this operation – see citation in appendices.

It was at this time towards the end of March, 1942 that 150 Brigade were moved from the position where we were at the top of the escarpment, northwards to the 150 Box at Gott el Ualeb which I have mentioned before. The whole Brigade had to go. We the Sappers were sent off to do something else first. I can't remember exactly what we had to do. It meant going into No-Man's Land again, a bit away from where we had been before, more to the south west, to examine some ex German minefields on the way and report on them, at a place called Bir Tengedden. We then went onto the south west, somewhere to the east I suppose of Rotunda Segnali which was to come into prominence not too much later when the German and Italian axis forces, Afrika Korps under Rommel, formed up round there to attack the Gazala Line from the south, instead of from the north and the west as expected and as they had done before.

Anyway we did whatever it was, and I really can't remember what it was that we had to do, but from there I received my orders to take myself and my section of Sappers to Bir Hacheim to start laying minefields there. So we got into our vehicles and we drove eastwards along the desert tracks by night mostly. That was a very easy, uneventful and delightful drive under stars, no sandstorms, no wind, lovely starlit nights, and one could find the way to Bir Hacheim really very easily indeed on this hard gravel desert by navigating on certain stars, getting a bearing on them and staying on the bearing for no longer than say 20 minutes, otherwise the degree of accuracy would be changed a bit because the star had moved. Anyway we got to Bir Hacheim and then got down to finding out what our orders were and what we had to do. This, as I have said before, was to lay approximately 10,000 mines in all around Bir Hacheim, as directed by the local commander.

The free French had not yet arrived at that particular moment, although we had heard that they were coming. I have told you earlier on about their arrival, about me being greeted by the coal black sergeant, blacker than the King of Spades, from the Troisième Battaillon de la Legion Etranger, and I have also told you about this remarkable dance to which I was invited at Bir Harmat. Originally before I knew that they had brought their girls with them all the way from Chad I said well I was a bit doubtful about going to a dance because I wasn't that sort of guy, but it all came right in the end, did it not?

So we laid the mines, and I handed them over to the French and then I moved back with the section to Gott el Ualeb to rejoin the rest of the Field Company and the Brigade, where we got on and on with more fortifications, more minefields round the Brigade position, more digging in of guns and so on. I remember the arrival of, I think it was the 42nd Royal Tank Regiment, who had Matilda tanks which were Infantry tanks with rather stouter guns on them than the previous tanks that we had had, and rather better guns than any anti tank weapons that were at that time available in the Brigade which were only 2 pounders. Life went on.

Gradually enemy activity started increasing. We were bombed by Stukas and we were being shelled at long distance, spasmodically, presumably by the Italian Artillery, who were good. Nothing really exciting and not all that dangerous either, until towards the end of May, and I guess it must have been the 26th, thereabouts, that the Battle of Gazala started. It was started by Rommel, as I have said, who came around from Rotunda Segnali, and outflanked the Gazala Line, which nobody ever believed he would do, by heading for Bir Hacheim and 150 Brigade. We were the two southerly parts of the Gazala defences, and he went round the bottom of Bir Hacheim, and came around the back to the east and got at the Gazala line from behind instead of from the front and this is what he proceeded to do.

Apart from the hook round the south end of Bir Hacheim the Arriete Division of the Italian Armour had been ordered to attack 150 Brigade on Gott el Ualeb directly through the minefield. I can't remember if it was Stepney Marsh or Hackney Marsh at that particular point. Anyway a squadron of the Arriete Division of Italian tanks came through and into whichever marsh it was in line abreast more or less. They were shot at by the 72nd Field Regiment guns, who were part of our Brigade group inside Gott el Ualeb Box. The Italians advanced about 2 miles into the mine marsh before hitting a belt of mines and the whole lot of them got onto this belt of mines and had a track or two tracks blown off their tanks, so there were 13 tanks stationary in the middle of the marsh.

I wasn't actually there to actually see that happen, but I am told that the Italian crews got out of their tanks pretty quick with their little suitcases in their hands and scarpered back through the minefield due westwards from whence they had come, leaving their tanks empty with broken tracks in the middle of the marsh. So they didn't stay to man their guns on their tanks, not that it would have done much good; but they didn't. So their tanks were empty of soldiery and anyway I was told to stop doing whatever it was that I was doing at the time, and to take a bunch of Sappers from my section and to destroy these tanks in the middle of the minefield. By destroy this meant to burn or otherwise make them totally useless as opposed to being recoverable, and possibly useful to the enemy at some later date.

Anyway Brigadier Haydon was the 150 Brigade Commander. He personally briefed me and told me what had happened and he ordered me to get on to the marsh as quickly as possible and do what I was told. So I took 10 Sappers with me, suitably armed with various bits of demolition equipment and stores, and on the way to the minefield I called on the 285th Battery Command Post to see my old friend Harry Clapham. He was the one that had been up the tower at Martuba with me and I asked him to give us artillery support if he saw us getting into trouble. Of course we had a good laugh about that.

The mine marsh then was about 3 miles deep I suppose, and the Italians had come through 2 miles of it, so I had about a mile to go or thereabouts from Harry Clapham's command post, through the wire marking the back of the minefield and into the minefield. We then had to walk through the minefield to get to the level of the mine belt along which the Italian Tank Squadron had blown themselves up. We got into the marsh via a secret lane which we had obviously marked on our maps, and if you kept within 5 yards left of a line especially marked with short angle iron pickets you were safe.

When we got down to the level of the belt we turned left, and still keeping an eye on where we were putting our feet we went out, and got amongst the tanks which were about 300 yards away from where we were. As I told you the crews had escaped and so the tanks were empty. I had never blown a tank up before but it didn't seem to be too difficult and I decided that the best way that we would do this job, the way the Brigadier wanted it, was to get into the turret of each tank, and to place mines which we had picked up from round and about and which obviously weren't going to be of any use again except as explosives, onto the commander's seats in each turret. So we did that and then we poured all the spare fuel that was carried on the tank in on top of this explosive, and then we connected all the tanks up together with detonating fuse. Having done that we got all our soldiers out of the way, and I lit the blue touch paper so to speak, and we buggered off, and the result was spectacular to say the least, and extremely noisy. As you can imagine not only were all the tanks, (in fact all the tanks but one) in flames, but the explosions inside also set off all the spare gun and machine gun ammunition inside, so it was real Paddy's night there!

So we reckoned that the job had been done and we returned to our line, getting ourselves out from the minefield the way we had come in and we were very pleased with ourselves indeed. We had a tremendous reception on coming back through the wire into our own area from the Infantry and from the Gunner Battery, who had been watching all this happening, and we really felt that this was not a bad way of starting a new battle, by destroying a complete squadron of tanks before breakfast, but as ever pride came before a fall. Something had gone wrong with the demolition circuitry in one of the tanks and that tank did not get blown up, so only 11 out of the 12 were complete wrecks. We were full of the joys of spring, and I repeated all this to the Brigadier in person, as he had briefed me in person, and he looked me straight in the eye and told me to go back and blow the final tank up. He was a great soldier, though I didn't really think so at the time, but I suppose he was right.

The next day was comparatively uneventful as far as I can remember. But the day when we did this lot was in fact my Dad's birthday, the 27th May, 1942, and by devious means he got to hear about it a few months later.

So we got back to carrying out normal sapper routine tasks including not only blowing up the leftover tank that the Brigadier had told me to do but we also blew up another one which we found somewhere else as a bonus. It had gone into somebody else's lines. So we really were extremely pleased with ourselves.

Before all this had happened my own personal vehicle which was an 8 cwt. Dodge truck had got severely damaged by being shot up by enemy aircraft and had to be disposed of. I was issued with a smaller but very practical vehicle which was a sort of small ambulance in a way, about the size now of a long wheel based Landrover. I was able to readjust the back with the aid of Squadron carpenters to a very handy vehicle which could be blacked out at night. You could sleep in it, you could also sit down four uncomfortably inside it and you could play bridge in the back. Indeed on some of our forays into the No man's land bit of the desert, particularly after looking for German mines and things at Bir Tengedden and Rotunda Segnali as I have described, we used to sit down in the back of my truck at night and play bridge. Well, there were three sergeants in my section. They were Sergeant Curling, MM, who won the Military Medal at Dunkirk I think, and he was a regular. He had been brought up as a proper regular sapper soldier. There was Sergeant Geordie Hopper who was the blacksmith in Gateshead or Barras Bridge, and then of course there was Lance Sergeant Lionel Longbottom who I have described before, who was the guy from whom I took all the credit for in surveying jobs in Cyprus earlier on the previous year. So making sure I got Lionel Longbottom as my partner because he was properly brought up and very intelligent and I was always a bad loser, we played together against Curling and Sergeant Hopper. We did normally win, not only because we played a better game, but because Sergeant Curling being a regular soldier always played his cards in order of seniority. I thought that was a little note I should put in.

I have also just remembered that on our way back from the raid on Martuba Airfield, I was somewhat on the flank of the main column, and coming up over one of the escarpments in the early light of dawn, I met a troop of armoured cars belonging, I think it was, to the 12th Lancers. So I stopped to chat to the Troop Commander and he said "Would you care to have breakfast?" I said, "Thank you very much but I've got some food with me." He said, "Well I've got a different sort of breakfast here." He had on offer gin and scrambled eggs if I would like them. I said thank you very much, what fun that was!

CHAPTER 9 - CAPTURE

It was on the morning of the 30th May that disaster struck. We were in our own lines, unprotected at the east side of the Brigade box, when we heard a mighty rumbling of enemy vehicles, tanks and armour, and on going forward to look over the bit of hill where we were, we could see enemy tanks with large crosses on them generally advancing in our direction from the wrong side, from the east instead of from the west, and we got back to the only means of communication we had which was a single telephone. We had no radio of any sort, just one telephone, back to Brigade HQ, and my OC at the time was Captain Gilly Thompson. He phoned and informed BHQ that we were being attacked by German Armour and we were told that it wasn't German Armour at all, it was the 21st Armoured Brigade, and we were not to worry. Well the fact of life was that it wasn't the 21st Armoured Brigade, it was parts of the 15th Panzer Division, or the 21st Panzer Division, or the 90th Light Division, all German Panzer troops or a mixture of vehicles and tanks from one or all of those three units. They came up to our lines over the small brow where we had no mines and no wire. The only anti tank defence we had was one single two pounder anti tank gun manned by a gunner subaltern and his crew, who did their best to shoot. I think they fired one shot before they were clobbered themselves. It's a well known fact that a 2 pounder anti tank gun does very little damage to a German Mark 4 tank which is what it was firing at. So we were overrun. Our total armament was that particular 2 pounder anti tank gun. We had 3 Boyes anti tank rifles, which I think I mentioned before in these notes, which weren't very much good against anything and that was it, and we were overrun and that was that. We were taken prisoner hande hoch.

We managed to burn the mine maps and so on before we left. We didn't leave anything valuable behind except a bit of money in the imprest account I think and we were taken away down the hill. Eventually we were loaded into captured vehicles and we were ignominiously taken back through Stepney Marsh, because the Germans had come right round the bottom and surprised the whole of the British army in the Gazala line and they had used up a lot of their ammunition and supplies. They were running out of fuel of one sort or another and they needed to get back to their side, if you like, the west side of the mined marshes, to recover, reform, rearm and get on with their battle. They did it by lifting the mines through Stepney Marsh, and where they made their minefield gap was not covered by any form of British fire. It was out of range of artillery and there were no infantry anywhere near, so what I said earlier about the laying of minefields and their value as a military weapon had come to pass. It depends on them being covered by fire. If they are not covered by fire the enemy can pick up the mines and do exactly what they like, and this is what they did.

Anyway we were taken in trucks, disarmed, as prisoners, through the gap onto their side, and eventually we came up to the water point in the general area of Tmimi which is near the Mediterranean coast, very tired and generally shattered. We probably hadn't eaten much that day. We certainly hadn't drunk much. We had no water, and although we still had our military equipment on, our water bottles were empty. We wanted to refill them but the Italians who were manning the water point would not allow us any water. They would only sell it for wrist watches, signet rings and that sort of thing. The Germans who were escorting us looked on in utter disgust at this extraordinary behaviour, because they were proper soldiers and the Sergeant in charge of our particular guards, if you like to call them that, outed his Mauser and shot the Italian sergeant stone dead and said: "Gentlemen, help yourselves." Funny story that, but true.

We were then moved on via Tmimi to a prison camp at Derna and then another prison camp at Barce. Then we were moved to Benghazi where we were embarked in Savoya 79 three engined Italian transport aircraft and flown across the Mediterranean to Lecce, where we spent a night or two in the tobacco factory as prisoners taunted by young women workers baring their bosoms and exhibiting their fannies through some windows on the other side of the street. Then we were embarked in vehicles again and sent up to Bari. What follows is my story from Bari onwards.

PART 2

ESCAPE FROM DURANCE VILE

CHAPTER 10 – PRISONER OF WAR

A friend advised me to start this story hanging by my thumbs from hooks on the ceiling of the deepest dungeon of the most impregnable fortress in Italy. In fact the dungeon was below ground level, but not the deepest of them all and I wasn't hanging by my thumbs, but it was the most impregnable fortress in Italy from the point of view of the prisoner of war inside trying to escape from it. It was called Campo di Concenttramento, numero 5. It was located at Gavi in Allessandria in an old Genoese fortress of which you can see a picture, and the prisoners inside were defined as "Ufficiale pericolosi e turbéulenti", which means prisoners who were dangerous or turbulent. I was not dangerous, but somewhat turbulent – just slightly.

I had been sent to Gavi from another P.O.W. camp called Bari after a couple of us had had an altercation with one of the staff of the camp there. It was in mid-afternoon some time in June 1942 with the sun blazing down that we observed a character strutting up and down outside the wire. He was an officer who was no more than 5 ft. and an Italian brick high. He had a high peaked cap with what appeared to be an old type Austin car badge at the front of it. He had a short but well-cut service dress tunic with what looked like 4 rows of the same medal above his breast, which he may well have earned, but he had riding breeches, beautifully pressed down the front, which seemed unfamiliar to us English from the hunting counties, and he had highly polished black field boots with, believe it or not zip fasteners up the back! This latter is what made him seem to us so hopeless, and what made us point at him across the wire as we doubled up in hysterical laughter. His reaction was instantaneous, and we were soon arrested by a squad of guards poking bayonets at us, and marched off to the cooler to await results. We did not wait very long before being marched into the Commandant's office, and lo and behold, there was the same character behind a large desk.... Through an interpreter he asked us what we had been laughing at, and when we said "You," he grabbed a brass bound ruler from his desk and started beating us about in fury. This display, though painful, made us even more hysterical with laughter, which didn't help much. Eventually and inevitably we were returned to the cooler and put on bread and water.

The camp at Bari was used really as a transit area for allied officer P.O.W's who had been captured by the German Afrika Corps in Libya. I never heard of anyone who had been captured by the Italians. However, with the capture of Tobruk, Bari became fuller and fuller, and the older inhabitants were moved to more permanent quarters. Those who were considered more dangerous or turbulent were moved to Camp 5 at Gavi and this included me. We were moved from Bari to Gavi, right up North, by special train.

I am now rather horrified to have to tell you the reason why the little bastard of a commandant at Bari was subsequently court martialled and shot by the Allies. This is hearsay, but apparently one of our number escaped by crawling under the wire at Bari, and was recaptured quite quickly. He was then forced by the commandant, at bayonet point, to demonstrate how and where he did it, and while doing so he was shot dead personally by the commandant for attempting to escape again. To be fair to the Italians that was the only incident of this nature that I have ever heard about, and on the whole we were properly treated according to the rules laid down in the Geneva Convention.

At Gavi, in the impregnable fortress, where I opened this tale, there was a splendid bunch of officer prisoners, much the same sort as would be found at Colditz I would imagine. Morale was very high, internal discipline of a high order, escaping continually being planned, food good and vino was plentiful.

I should mention here that the Geneva Convention's rules on feeding was that prisoners should be fed at the same basic rate as the soldiers of the country which was holding them prisoner. As we were prisoners of the Italians and the Italian soldiers were given half a litre of vino every day as part of their ration we were therefore entitled to that as well. Although we never actually received all of it, we practically always received some, so it was possible to lay in large stores of vino for some future happy occasion when we could all get thoroughly pissed.

There was one splendid Royal Canadian Engineer Officer at Gavi that I remember very well. He was called Jeff Jowitt, and he was taken prisoner after the first allied parachute operation of WW 2 on the Trajino Aquaduct near Naples. He would flog everything he had – food, clothes, cigarettes and all to buy more vino, and when he reckoned he had an adequate quantity he would slowly become stoned. During this process he would shout abuse at his guards who stayed remarkably tolerant. They only arrested and despatched him to the cooler for his own health, and so as not to disturb us other peaceful characters. We naturally protested about this and retained as much grog as we could for him until he was released again.

Surprisingly, looking back on it, it was with some reluctance that I left Gavi for a place called Padula in the middle of Italy, way down south of Salerno. The reason that a bunch of us were moved was because we weren't considered dangerous, only turbulent, and by then there were a lot more dangerous officers around than us, and they required more rigorous confinement.

Anyway, off we went, marched out of the impregnable fortress, down to the railway station and away south, down to Genoa, along the Ligurian Riviera, and on south through Livorno and Roma. We travelled in relative comfort in passenger carriages with a guard in each compartment, plus two guards in each corridor and an officer per two carriages. In any one compartment there were just about nine of us and a guard. This was about July, 1942 and there was no Allied bombardment of the Italian railways then and trains maintained normal speeds. There was no chance whatever of escaping through the carriage windows, and the guards knew this. Our guard went to sleep somewhere near Grossetto, and the least we felt we could do was to remove his rifle from between his legs, open the window, throw the rifle out, close the window and all go to sleep again. When he awoke, there was a look of bewilderment on his face, and he started kind of patting his pockets to see where his wallet had gone. We asked what the matter was, and he said that he couldn't find his rifle. So we said "what an extraordinary thing", and we helped him search for it under the seats and under all our kit in the luggage racks, under the cushions, in the corridor and everywhere, but he never found it. I wonder what happened to him in the end.

I vaguely recollect stopping in Rome in the dark and thinking of making a break for it and heading for Vatican City, but I didn't and nor did anyone else at that time. Anyway, the next day we arrived at the Certosa San Lorenzo at Padula in Salernitano, surely one of the most beautifully built monasteries in Italy. It had been used as a P.O.W camp in WW1 as we discovered when we were searching for ways to escape from it, and it was being used as such again. It was Campo di Concentramento, numero 35 in WW2. It housed 500 officer prisoners plus about 80 other rank prisoners and was protected by about 600 guards. What a compliment, having one each!

I will try and describe the monastery in some detail so that you can understand subsequent efforts to get out of it, and you will see a photograph of the set up, and the quadrangle on the right. The size of it is 3 acres, no less, and so you can see that it was a pretty formidable place. I will describe it further in a bit more of this tale later on.

It was here that I met Tony Payn for the first time, and it is about him and with him that much of the middle of this story is concerned. Those of you who are interested in this sort of story will probably have read many similar ones where the daily routine of life in a P.O.W. camp is described much better than I can do – the hopes and the fears and the discomforts and occasionally the relative comforts, the living at very close quarters with the essential give and take that goes with that, the snippets of real news that occasionally arrive with a new prisoner or when we got the radios working, the arrival of mail and parcels from home, the arrival of Red Cross food parcels, the drinking parties when possible, the play acting, the music making, the continual efforts of many to escape, and the efforts of a very few to prevent people escaping so that they could live in such comfort as they had, leaving us to carry on with trying to escape.

We remember the cold, we remember the heat, we remember baiting the guards, we remember the food such as it was, sometimes plentiful and sometimes not, the debates, the lectures, the courses of everything from wines to learning a bit more classical history, the gambling, the games outside and inside, the occasional glimpses of the local world outside on heavily escorted marches, and punishments when we behaved wrongly.

Of course we were about 100% luckier to be incarcerated in Italy than those in Germany, and at least 1,000% better off than those who got caught by the Japanese.

So in hindsight there wasn't too much to grumble about – but human nature being what it is, and being essentially selfish, you had to exist in the environment in which you found yourself. If you had any sense at all you made the best of it. For those who were married with or without kids at home it must have been ten times worse than for those of us who were not. Our parents must have worried far more than we did ourselves.

Most of us lived for the moment of regaining freedom and about half of the rest of us tried to do something towards that end. It kept us busy, it kept us relatively fit, it kept us tired so that we slept well either by day or night depending upon when we were on shift or on watch helping others to do the same thing. There were many who for some reason or another did not wish to or couldn't escape and of those number were great citizens who could use their wits or their particular expertise, skill or something to help the rest. There were tailors, map makers, forgers, linguists, cooks, radio experts and many who were bloody minded enough to create diversions and general mayhem when required just for the joy of living and helping others.

One of the things that kept us endlessly busy and amused was making sure that the opposition in the shape of our guards never had it all their own way. There was a particular case in point when it was announced that a very senior General was to inspect us tomorrow and that we were to be on our very best behaviour or else something drastic would happen to us. We were lined up in our usual five groups of a hundred, each group in five lines of twenty, with an armed sentry on the right and left flank of each group. We were formed up like this every day, every morning and every evening for roll call or Apello as it was called, and it was preceded by bugles being blown. We formed up under one of the long colonnades or ambulatories round the courtyard where the monks used to wander around meditating, and off which some of the monks' quarters lay. On this particular occasion with the General coming it was a fine day, and we were all there lined up properly and behaving particularly well when the great General in person walked down the cloister from the Italian part of the monastery with the Commandant. It must have been a very great disappointment to him to see that the first and right hand Italian soldier on the right of the first group of one hundred prisoners had an apple stuck on the end of his bayonet. How it got there of course nobody quite knew!

Two other special parades were ones which most of us will remember well. The first of these was, so far as I can recollect, in the Autumn of 1942, when a dozen or so prisoners escaped after dark. How they got out and where they were going doesn't matter much, but it was incumbent on all of us to give them the best possible start, and for their identities to be covered up for as long as possible, so that the fact that they had escaped, and subsequently when they were discovered, nobody would know exactly who they were. Therefore the descriptions couldn't be sent round the local police and military authorities.

I think they got out at about 8 p.m. We had to be in bed with lights out by 10 p.m. Naturally there were dummies in the beds of all the absentees, sometimes not actually in the beds because somebody live might be sleeping there and the dummy would be in his bed just to confuse. Anyway at 1 a.m. the following morning our masters had discovered that something was seriously amiss. The alarm bells rang and the bugles blew and the lights went on and squads of soldiers appeared with fixed bayonets looking very fierce indeed, and we were ordered down for a roll call. Naturally, knowing what was at stake, we took the maximum time to comply, and it wasn't until about 2 a.m., an hour later, that we eventually all got down to the appointed place. In fact we didn't all go to our appointed places which made the chaos more chaotic. A number took down with them mattresses, chairs, blankets, playing cards, even a table to play bridge on in the uncertain light – and so on and so forth.

There was much noise and threatening language amongst our guards and their officers and the sound of machine guns being cocked in the courtyard. Eventually it was coming on first light before they could count us properly, let alone know who it was who had scarpered. They couldn't actually get the number who had scarpered exactly right because of one or two tricks we had invented for ghost numbers to be present or absent, of which more anon. So when dawn broke they knew that 10, 11 or 12 prisoners had escaped, but they didn't really know who they were. So it was then decided that we would each be marched off and marked one by one to go through an interrogation screen against our documents. We were asked questions about our relatives, our mother, father, grandparents, wives, how many children we had, where we were captured etc. etc., and like good soldiers we replied with what honesty the occasion merited. It took in all some 13 hours for our masters to establish the facts, which had given the escapers some 18 hours fair start. Sadly they were all picked up eventually. Most of them landed up at Gavi in the "periculoso" category. The second special parade which caused great laughter to us and enormous frustration to our protectors I'll let you know about later on. But there were other things that went on in that context.

One instance was caused by guard carelessness, which was a fairly rare event. The iron gate, which separated our part of the monastery from the open patch where we were allowed to walk and play games, was locked every day at sunset. The old outside wall of the monastery in fact went round part of this open patch at some distance from the monastery of course, and there were guard posts with searchlights and machine guns built on top. Anyway at about 8 p.m. one balmy spring evening, we heard the noise of shooting from the direction of the games' patch, and we rushed to the few windows that overlooked it. To our astonishment we saw the figure of one of our Carabinieri, who were really smarter and better disciplined guards, who did internal guard duties. He was lying on the ground lit up by searchlights being shot at. He was clearly a brave man but also bloody angry. He took out his small Beretta automatic from its holster and started shooting back at the guards. In the event there were no casualties in this engagement, and we reckoned it ceased because of the cheering coming from us who were observing the operation. The wretched fellow had apparently been doing his rounds checking that everything was locked up, found the iron gate wasn't, so he wandered outside possibly to have a quick smoke before going back to lock it. We were able subsequently to ask our internal guards innocent questions about their safety for a week or two after that, and also their standard on the ranges. It was all good for morale. When we were able to draw the attention of one of the Italian officers to the sight of one of the external sentries masturbating on duty in daylight, that was really terrific.

CHAPTER 11 – SEWER RATS

In spite of these two examples the general standard of our guarding was fairly high, and by sheer weight of numbers the chances of getting away with a break overtly were fairly small. There were at any one time some 200 opposition to look after the 580 of us, so generally speaking, for larger groups to escape it had to be done by covert means, tunnels and so forth.

In a group as large as this there obviously had to be very close control on escape plans, and like in any other P.O.W. camp there was an escape committee responsible for this coordination. Tony Payn and I only had one meeting with them. We'd been doing extensive reconnaissances of the means of getting out and had decided that tunnelling was not particularly convenient for us as we lived upstairs in the top ambulatory of the old monks' cells which you can see in the photograph above the colonnades. But there was a network of sewers, some new, but mostly very old ones, which definitely bore further investigation, and what we wanted from the escape committee was really the exclusive rights to the sewers and these we were granted. What a great honour!

The point about the sewers, we thought, was that they would undoubtedly be as much and indeed more under the Italian part of the camp as they would be under the part occupied by us. The old monks' cells with their garden compounds going out towards the wall would have had their own long drop arrangements unconnected to a main system and therefore only the communal parts of the monastery would be linked up to the sewers, like the kitchens, the refectory, the area round the library and so on.

We of course had to have an entry point in our part of the camp, and this we found easily enough under a manhole cover which was downstream of the British soldiers' latrines and the communal bath house. Italian drainage is still not good at the best of times, and there didn't seem to be all that much room down there for both it and us. Anyway, we did have the exclusive rights, so we decided we might as well make use of them. The first 60 yards or so were really quite disgusting, because not only were we crawling through the early source of what is euphemistically called the effluent, but this was here and there cross plumbed in a way that forced you to either climb over the cross plumbing or at worst go under it, and we didn't have wet suits, we didn't have masks, and we didn't have oxygen. All we had were the exclusive rights. This particular sewer got deeper and deeper in it and clearly wasn't going to get us anywhere. But we had noticed on the way down an old and small rectangular side sewer about 20 yards away from our entry point. After 2 or 3 days we decided to investigate.

It was quite short, about 10 yards long, dry, and slightly downhill from where we entered, and at its end was a slab of rock with a hole of about 10" diameter knocked through it that must have taken ancient effluent into something underneath that you couldn't see properly. We had to do something about it, and there wasn't anything else to do but acquire a hammer and cold chisel to enlarge the hole. When in prison there isn't an easy access to a B & Q Hardware store. On the other hand there are a hell of a lot of nice guys around all minding their own business, and one particular bunch of these who were working on a deep deep tunnel, of which you will hear more anon., just happened to have acquired a hammer and cold chisel off one of the Italian masons who had been in to repair something. Whether they got them by bartering cigarettes or just by plain stealth I have no idea, but they got them and happily lent them to us.

There's one thing you can't prevent when using such tools on solid rock, and that is noise. We reckoned that we were only a couple of feet underground, and that we were approximately under the end of the refectory but we were just still on our side of the camp. Luckily the refectory was used not only for eating in by all of us, but also for stage productions, for music making, for band concerts, choral society and the like. So it wasn't too difficult to get some of the above to make one hell of a noise for a couple of hours one afternoon while we enlarged the hole to get our then slim and youthful bodies through to whatever was below. Why we were never discovered doing this I'll never know, because from time to time our efforts below were not exactly in unison with those above, but we did it and we got away with it.

What was in fact below us was a medium to dry sewer of arched construction, some 6 foot high at the peak, and it was clear that such effluent as there was from our kitchen waste, came from our end. There wasn't any effluent from the Italian side to start with anyway. Our end was to the left as you drop through the hole in the rock. To the right and not very far down on the right, we came across a new concrete block, rectangular in shape, which allowed the kitchen effluent underneath and the air to circulate through the arch at the top. It had very clearly been put there by far seeing Italians to prevent the British escaping through the sewers. We had by then got very excited by the prospect, and having got so far were damned if we were going to be defeated by a mere concrete block, but we had to assume that if our guards had put it there they both had the means and the intent to inspect it from time to time to see if all was well. We discovered that near it on their side of the camp was a manhole for doing just this – so the conversation went roughly like this:

"What the hell are we going to do about that concrete block, Pissy?"

(Pissy was the nickname of my friend Tony Payn.)

He said, "We'll knock the bloody thing down of course."

"But supposing the Ities find the block knocked down?"

"Well," he said, "they won't know because we will have replaced it with a carbon copy."

So we had to measure it, decide its colour and texture, and settle down to make a carbon copy through which we could pass fairly easily if ever we managed to knock the original down. We also had to make it in such a way that we could carry it through the original manhole, through 20 yards of effluent, sometimes over or sometimes under any interfering plumbing. Then we had to carry it left along the dry sewer and take it through the hole that we had made to get ourselves through the rock into the sewer underneath. Then we had to knock the concrete block down, and replace it with this copy which had to look exactly like the original, and it all had to be done on the same day, or at least the latter part of it had to be done on the same day, in case of inspection.

We realised that we needed help and as our efforts progressed, our sewer gang increased to a total of 12 people, whose names I sadly can't remember, plus of course an upstairs party to decontaminate us after each emergence from the last terrible 20 yards. But first things first – we had to design and make the phony concrete block. In fact this proved far less difficult than we had imagined. It was easy enough to find lengths of wood from fruit boxes. Similarly nails could be made from the same source. Somebody had some spare pieces of chicken wire which he'd nicked. I think they'd been used for covering early vegetables cultivated in one of the monks' cells. There was some spare cement about, and also some lime. Water was no problem, and nor was sand. Backing for the chicken wire was no problem either because of the quantity of used Red Cross cardboard boxes. Hinges and screws were a bit more difficult, but the former could be made out of wire, and an adequate substitute for nails could also be made from wire.

It didn't in fact take much more than a day to gather together the materials and not more than another to knock the folding framework together. It had to fold to get it through the hole in the rock, but we had of course the necessary batons and nails to strengthen it when we erected it in the big sewer underneath. The next day we took all this stuff underground and stored it by the big sewer and on the following day we went below for the big event. We once more borrowed the heavy hammer and chisel, and once again organised the band for a major rehearsal in the refectory up above. This I remember included the Anvil Chorus by Verdi, from, I imagine, "Il Trovatore". The concrete block almost fell apart in our hands. It was far less difficult dealing with it than making that hole through the rock. We sized and fitted the phony block consisting of the chicken wire door on hinges, complete with catch, and then plastered the whole thing up, so that even at more than a casual glance you couldn't tell it from the original. All this was a full day's work, and the band above complained that their breath was short. Amazingly our guards must have suspected nothing at all because nothing whatsoever happened. We left our new device fallow, so to speak, for a couple of days to await events, but there weren't any. So we went down again to discover what wonders there were beyond.

And wonders there were indeed. The big sewer to which we had gained entrance went on for about 80 - 100 yards. If you had been a Sicilian type Italian with a smaller type of rifle, you could have fixed your bayonet and marched down the sewer in the slope arms position. You would have caught your bayonet on odd stones projecting from the arch above here and there, but only if you had to duck, but of course talking of ducks, I had duck's disease and didn't have to, but Pissy Payn and some of our fellow sewer rats had to.

The sewer had a longish full quarter bend to the left towards the end of it. Although the bend was the wrong way round it had to be called Regent Street, and I'm sure that Austin Reed and the Goldsmiths and Silversmiths would have entirely approved. What more appropriate than arriving in Piccadilly Circus, and there it was, right in front of us – an underground roundabout with roughly the right number of streets emanating from it.

I have been back there since and inspected the property, much to the surprise of the current landlord, when I demanded entry to the monastery of which he was the custodian. I took my wife and family with me as witnesses to an astonishing visit, for which we have as a memento at home one of the bricks that was later to give us so much trouble.

Piccadilly Circus had, as added space, the bottom of a fountain that graced a delightful little colonnaded piazza in the real centre of the monastery, but we weren't to know that. Straight ahead was Lower Regent Street, Piccadilly to the right, and Coventry Street to the left. Because the shortest way to freedom was by our calculations down Lower Regent Street, we decided to investigate that first, but it all seemed to get blocked up, presumably to prevent us falling down the Duke of Yorks' step. No go.

So then we tried Piccadilly, which was very much more promising. In the distance you could see light at the end of the tunnel. So we crawled down it with enormous care and in total silence because by then we were well under the Italian part of the monastery. Payn was leading and I was a yard or two behind him when suddenly there was a loud plop and a splash. It was around about 11 o'clock in the morning which was clearly the time when someone was doing his daily devotions. By careful calculation we worked out later that at that particular moment of time Payn was exactly underneath the Commandant's personal long drop, and long it was, something like 50 foot I should think. There's an expression in English about being shat on from a great height, and this was it.

In spite of this battle honour, we pressed on silently towards the light, but the effluent got deeper and deeper. Eventually we had to agree that Piccadilly was no go also, so we had to hope that Coventry Street would come up trumps and we set off there the following day. In fact Coventry Street was dry or dryish anyway, just rather full of black, slimy and rather large rats. It too was blocked, but this time not with modern concrete, but with solid earth and rubble put there personally by the monks some hundreds of years before. On the right there was another of those small rectangular dry sewers above the level of the main sewer, so we got into that.

This was very much crawling only and about 10 or 12 yards down it was what looked like a brick wall built not quite up to roof height which prevented further progress. On further examination we found a manhole cover immediately above the brick wall, so we must have been almost at ground level again and squinting over the brick wall we would again see light in the distance. This was very exciting indeed as we reckoned that the light was coming from outside the monastery altogether, and that therefore if we could remove the intervening brickwork we might be out and away.

In the next few days we were examining the problem and we discovered two more things of great importance to us. The first was that if you happened to be lying up against the wall at 1 p.m. you could hear the radio news emanating from somewhere up above, and it wasn't just the Italian lunchtime news broadcast, it was the Allied propaganda broadcast, called "La Voce d'Italia", coming from North Africa. Clearly we must be underneath some Italian officer's quarters.

The other discovery was that heavy boots occasionally walked across the manhole cover above us and sometimes actually stopped on the cover, so we were clearly below a sentry beat of sorts. We subsequently found out that we were underneath, or more or less underneath, the Italian officer's mess. Well, these extraordinary discoveries led us to two conclusions. The first and most obvious was that the removal of the brickwork and there were about 20 bricks to be removed as we thought, would have to be done in total silence, as the sentry's feet were often only 15" away.

CHAPTER 12 – RELIEF FROM THE DAILY GRIND

The second was that Tony Payn, who spoke fluent Italian, and I, who were anyway paired off as one of the six shifts of two people in the sewer gang would always have to be present at l p.m. in order to listen to the news. I didn't understand a word of Italian in those days, except that "si" meant "yes". It wasn't until several days after I finally escaped that I discovered that the Italian for "no" was "no". Tony however had got damaged when the Wellington in which he was second pilot had force landed in Sicily some 18 months before, and while being sorted out in hospital, he had learnt Italian grammatically and fluently, the latter I think through chatting up his nurses, as he was always a great hand at that.

Well, to take the second thing first, we would take off for our shift at 11a.m. It took 15 minutes to negotiate the sewers from our entry point as far as the brick wall. We were able to do about 1 ½ hours brick loosening, and then Payn, with pencil and paper ready, would take note of the news from 1 ⏹ 1.15 p.m. We would then return, and during our decontamination, he would dictate the news in English to a stenographer, who would then type it, and post it on the camp notice board by 1.45 p.m. Great crowds would come and read it, often cheering wildly on hearing of another desert victory, and inevitably our guards soon found out, and not unnaturally assumed that we had an illicit radio. We had of course worked that one out in advance, and through the camp organisation, we had arranged that something that really looked like a radio should be constructed out of used tins from Red Cross parcels, and should be carefully, but relatively obviously, hidden. We never in fact had much problem in really hiding things properly if we wanted to.

Sure enough the chief ferret and his gang of fellow ferreters became very active indeed, and one fine day there was a snap roll call in the afternoon. Lots of guards with fixed bayonets about the place urging us on parade, but we couldn't be too quick as people had to get back from their tunnelling or other sewage works, and get cleaned up. Well we did all get on parade in about ½ an hour or so, and we were counted, and we were all there. Then the Italian Commandant made an entrance and stood in front of us and sent for the chief ferret who arrived in front of us all waving the fake radio above his head. I need hardly say that we cheered his dramatic entrance to the echo. It was a great boost to morale. Of course the next day the news was posted on the board at 1.45 p.m. precisely once again, so they knew we had a proper radio somewhere, because how else could we have done this? It must have caused them all a persistent and nagging pain.

Our dress for sewer bashing was a pair of shorts and a pair of P.T. shoes. This was the minimum consistent with comfort and safety and also reduced the cleaning up problem to the minimum. Tony and I had a splendid soldier called Jack Occlestone to look after us. He was a Liverpudlian whose parents ran a pub overlooking Aintree racecourse. He used to say that when the war was over, he would ask us along on National Day, and we would sit on the roof of the pub, and we'd have a pulley and rope, and pull up buckets and buckets of beer. I don't know what happened to him in the end, but at that time he looked after our problems above ground, and was of course on the list to escape with us when we went.

He also helped us tremendously in our more legal duties of being Wing Wine Officer, and Assistant Wing Wine officer, a job which Tony and I took very seriously indeed. As already mentioned we were all entitled to a basic soldier's ration, provided such rations were available. Sometimes they didn't seem to amount to much. During a bad but luckily fairly short period in the hard winter of 1943 the ration came to 50gms of bread and one apple a day as a personal issue, plus some skilly with one square of meat the size of four sugar lumps per week, all cooked centrally.

There was pretty well always vino, and the minimum ration according to the Italian army scales was ½ a litre per man per day. This was regarded also as a personal issue but it obviously had to be controlled. There were 400 of us living in the upstairs cloisters and 100 in the monks⬚ cells below around the courtyard. For purposes of administration upstairs was split into 4 units or wings, and downstairs one unit, all of 100 each, and with 80 soldiers on top of that, it made up to 6 wings. Everybody watched the distribution of wine like hawks, because there was a lot you could do with wine. You could drink it, or you could save it, or you could use it for barter. You could drink it cold, or you could mull it. You could even with a few additions try and distil it. It was usually fairly disgusting. It really was red infuriator. Tony and I and a few of our friends sleeping around about us reckoned it was best to save it up and have it in great quantity mulled. In the Red Cross parcels there were raisins and sugar, and using them and the first peelings in season, you could produce quite a brew. Jack Occlestone used to do this for us on occasions and of course assist us to knock it back. A great anaesthetic from time to time it was, and well worth the subsequent hangovers.

The main point about having the arduous duty of being the wine officers was that you were entitled to the swipes, and for every 50 litres distributed, there was usually about a litre of swipes. So Payn, Cowtan and Occlestone, although sometimes they went a bit short of food, never really suffered too much from thirst whilst in Padula, nor later on as we shall discover.

CHAPTER 13 – THE LAST BRICK

Back to the brickwork which was preventing our further progress. It was, we thought, a drain of sorts, three bricks thick at the bottom and two separated bricks at the top. What was involved in removing it was separating brick from brick without making any noise at all in case the sentry was adjacent or even immediately overhead. This meant that each brick had to be drilled between the mortar and the brick itself and then levered off. This in turn meant that we had to design special tools to do this and then get them down to the quarry face, if you like, to see if they worked. Of course all this took time. The brick was of solid bake and very hard, as indeed was the mortar, and nothing short of a well tempered metal tool, pointed at the end, would get into it.

We got hold of a bit of steel reinforcing bar through our friends, and after having set up a kind of blacksmith's forge in the camp kitchen, produced a tool with a squarish point at one end and a handle at the other end and tempered the squarish point. It had to be a square point rather than a round one so that it would bite into the brick work. Then we thought we would have to lubricate the point as it went into the brickwork, both to assist the cutting and to silence it a bit. This was very simply done by filling a small tin with cooking oil and making a wick out of woven pyjama cord which hung out of the bottom of the tin. You placed this on top of the brick being worked on and let the oil drip on the point of the drill.

The last real problem was leverage, or how to separate a brick from its neighbour silently, once you thought you had drilled into it far enough. Bearing in mind that you were lying flat on your face, or at best on your side, you couldn't produce much leverage with your arm. There simply wasn't room enough. So it had to be produced by an artificial fulcrum, and we were lucky enough to get, from the same inexhaustible source of hammers, chisels and so on, a steel wood wedge, one of those heavy triangular bits of metal that you split timbers with.

If you put a loose brick or two on the floor of the dry sewer and you put the wood wedge on top, in between the loose brick and your drilling tool, stuck into the hole that's already made, and then you gently bang the end of the wood wedge, the solid brick will become separated from the mortar. Because this operation might be a bit noisy, and you are worried about the sentry being perhaps only 15" above you, you quieten everything down by wrapping a piece of material round the end of the wedge. You lose a bit of force by so doing but you definitely gain silence. Well, it worked! But it was a very slow operation indeed, and it took all six shifts three days to move two bricks. And as there were some 20 bricks to move, we were talking about a month's work, but slowly, slowly as the bricks were loosened and removed, we could see that our calculations were right and that freedom lay ahead.

The danger of discovery from above was always there of course, but we had taken maximum precautions against this. What was really unpleasant down there was the unwitting attentions of one or two of the huge black sewer rats, who would come tearing down over the brickwork, down one's naked back, and your fellow shift worker's, and away. But familiarity bred contempt, and we even got used to that sort of treatment.

So there came the time when we could report to the senior British officer of the camp the estimated date of our departure and how many people we thought we could get through the tortuous, and to some of them, totally unfamiliar exit route. There were 12 of us plus Jack Occlestone and 2 other soldiers who had helped us in various ways, which made 15 certainties, plus a number of deserving and some less deserving ones. We didn't think we could get more than an absolute maximum of 18 people out on the first attempt. There were tremendous problems with getting through the labyrinth with all the clothing, food and so on that we needed, remembering that we were doing all the work dressed in practically nothing at all. There was the problem of timing, because it would have to be done at night after the last roll call, with all the attendant difficulties of insufficient lighting and so on. So 18 was a fairly optimistic figure, and we had to put an order of priority into that of course.

At this stage we were asked what our individual plans were to be when we finally got out, and we were also let in on the secret details of a major tunnel being constructed from the bottom of a 36 ft. deep well at the back of one of the monks' walled gardens. This in fact was being done by our friends, who seemed to have all the kit in the world, and who produced from somewhere practically everything we were short of.

The senior British officer's idea, no doubt advised by the escape committee, was that we should time our exits to be simultaneous. The tunnel, which was probably a far greater feat of clandestine engineering than ours', was likely to take a little bit longer to complete than our route, but not all that much. Apart from anything else after it had safely passed under the odd anti tunnelling ditch around the perimeter defences, and maybe the odd sound detector that we didn't personally know about it had to come up 36 ft. to reach ground level, but the great and obvious advantages of using the two means of exit simultaneously were twofold. First, that at least double the number would probably get out on night one, in fact possibly more, as the tunnel route was somewhat less complicated than ours, and second that the subsequent Italian hue and cry, the ferreting, the searching, and the rest, might well be satisfied when it had uncovered just one of the two exits. After a quiet period while frayed Italian tempers returned to normal the exit that hadn't been found could be used again, or so we hoped.

Anyway it was a great idea and one we felt bound to agree with, and we timed our operations accordingly. We paid a great deal of attention at this stage to getting on with our personal preparations in detail. There were clothes to make; the senior British officer had insisted that we must wear caps, whether to preserve the Sandhurst image of British officers or what, we were not quite sure. I was dragged up at Woolwich, and Pissy was from Cranwell. Mine was made from a pair of hound's tooth checked slippers sent out to me by my mother. I don't suppose Herbert Johnson would have been too proud of it, but it satisfied the S.B.O. and that was all that mattered for the moment. The way we approached the problem of clothing was geared to what we proposed to do when we got out.

We thought anyway that the chances of us being mistaken for Italians were limited, and provided we weren't using the roads or railways, which we didn't propose to do, and provided we were intending to walk by night, and hide up by day, that our outward appearance really didn't matter too much. What was far more important was to be able to carry the things we needed, like food, with the minimum of bother.

No disguises were really necessary for our particular group of four as our situation and intention was to steal a transport aircraft, either a German Junkers 52 or an Italian Savoya 79, and fly it to Malta, waving one of our not so white underpants out of the parachuting door to avoid being shot down by either unfriendly Beau fighters of the Royal Air Force, or unfriendly Royal Artillery anti-aircraft gunners on Malta. Pissy was a bomber pilot as you already know, and Abie Goldie was a Beau fighter pilot. They at least had 2 engines. Abie had been talked into joining us sewer rats partly because he was a great man, partly because he occupied a fairly adjacent bed to ours', but really because we wanted him because of his skill and ability as a pilot, and because of his enormous and unfailing sense of humour.

One of our fellow prisoners was a Swede who had joined the Royal Air Force before World War 2, and he had flown transport aircraft for Swedish airlines, S.A.S. He knew exactly what to do with a Junkers 52 and had somehow acquired detailed knowledge of the Savoya 79. I suppose there wasn't too much difference. What he was able to do was to explain in detail to the professional pilots, i.e. Pissy and Abie, what the cockpit and takeoff drill was, and they in turn could explain to us novices what we would have to do as crewmen, like in those days chock drill, and climbing up the ladder pretty fast afterwards, let alone later doffing our underwear as recognition signals.

The military airfield which we proposed to raid and from which we proposed to remove our escape "ve-hicle" as the Americans would have described it, was on the coast and as the crow flies almost exactly 200 kilometres due west of us over an Apennine or two. When you are crossing mountains on foot you have to at least double the map distance which meant that we had to allow for 400 kilometres or 250 miles of walking. We reckoned that at night in June and July of high summer we had about 8 hours darkness plus

1 hour half light, (give or take) and that therefore at an average of 2 m.p.h. including losing our way and halts for tiredness, excitement, fright and so on that we might take 10 days to a fortnight walking. This sounds absurd but later on we were to prove it wasn't, and that we had got our facts just about right.

We had found out or been advised that the form on Italian aerodromes was that aircraft were refuelled on landing, and then put out to dispersal areas by day or night, well separated to minimise damage by Allied air attacks. This meant that we expected to break through the perimeter wire of the airfield we were aiming for without too much difficulty because there were unlikely to be sufficient guards to prevent us from doing so. Anyway, they wouldn't be expecting such an entrance. With the aircraft at dispersal there wouldn't be too much difficulty in getting into one, particularly at night, and with the experts present, to get organised to fly it off at an appropriate time, wind and weather permitting. The SBO accepted this plan without any demur at all, because at least we had equipped ourselves with proper head gear. So far as us 4 were concerned plus Jack Occlestone we were all set to go.

In the meantime it had become very obvious to the Italians that their country was about to be invaded. It was July, 1943 and the Allies had completed the conquest of North Africa and were clearly set to get on with the invasion of Europe. In all probability Italy would be the next objective, and it was highly likely that as a preliminary step it would be necessary for them to clear Sicily, thus relieving Malta, and providing good seaports from which to occupy the Southern part of Italy and to establish bases sufficiently far forward for aircraft to operate from further northwards. Presumably, we thought, there would be airborne and seaborne landings much further north, say in Genoa or La Spezia and on the other side of the plain at Rimini, Ravenna, that area, in order to cut off Italy completely, or the leg if you like of Italy, and thus reduce the country to almost total submission and prevent much German resistance south of the Alps.

In the event the latter didn't happen, but the threat of it happening decided the Italians, as a very minor detail, to move any Allied prisoners they had in the south to somewhere further north. So far as we were concerned, they timed everything absolutely perfectly for themselves in their duty as our guards. They moved us just a week before we were leaving voluntarily. We had one brick remaining in the sewer which had to be removed, and the principal tunnel gang had only about 12 ft. left of their uphill cut to complete their exit. There are other details about what happened during that time but the fact was that we were unable to carry out our plans. So we never did escape from Padula, but our great endeavours, despite our bitter disappointment, stood us in very good stead later.

John Cowtan Pissy Payn (3rd from left) with Don Enrico, other POWs and partisans

John Cowtan and Giuseppe Baldini

Padula Monastery

Padula Monastery, POW bedrooms.

Campo di Concenttramento, numero 5, Gavi, Allessandria

John Cowtan and Guiseppe Baldini in front of statue of the priest Don Enrico Porcignone

Searching for the last brick at Padula Monastery in 1960

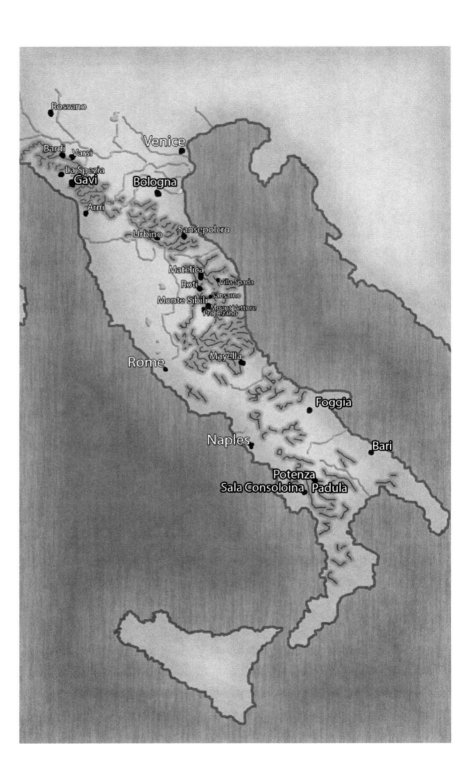

CHAPTER 14 – JOURNEY TO BOLOGNA

We were told that we would be moving at short notice and that we should pack up any kit that we had. In fact we had a great deal of kit, and we wanted to take everything we had with us, particularly our escaping material, so to be as well equipped as possible for getting out of wherever we might be going next. We didn't know until we were on our way that this was going to be Bologna.

We had received on repayment in the previous six months a wooden box each, somewhat like an old midshipman's chest, to store our personal kit in. As you can imagine you don't get captured with a packed suitcase all ready to go, unless you happen to be an Italian. Our clothing etc. didn't amount to much, but all the escaping kit amounted to a great deal, and certainly had to be carefully packed, even if we might lose it eventually. There were hammers and trowels and drills and saws and a miscellany of bits of metal which might come in useful for something. There were keys, oil tins, oil, string, compasses, maps, money and so on. There were 70 yards of double electric flex complete with lampholders, bulbs and adaptors of various sorts, to plug into the camp supply. There was food of all sorts, in particular our cooked battle buns, heavy and hard, made of baked chocolate, sugar, condensed and powdered milk, margarine and raisins etc. from Red Cross parcels, and of course my cap. This was most important as the S.B.O. was coming with us.

So we packed everything up as tactically as we knew how, using false bottoms that we had built into our chests for the more valuable stuff, and hoping for the best with the rest. Indeed we were hoping for the best all round with everything. The chests were all stacked up to be removed by lorry to the station, and we weren't to see them again until we got to Bologna, but as I have said we didn't know we were going there until later. This left us still despondent and pondering our fate and naturally all those intending to escape were discussing how and where they would do it on the train. Were we going to be in cattle trucks or carriages? How did you unlink trucks or carriages from one another on a slope? And how the hell did you put the brakes on having done so? And what was the minimum kit you needed with you to make an escape attempt?

We were paraded in the early morning and marched off to the station and into a fairly civilised train with carriages and a corridor, much as we had travelled in before. Eventually it took off northwards through Sala Consolina, somewhere near Potenza, heading, someone thought, for Foggia in the plains on the Adriatic side. Progress was slow and bumpy, and two very sporting Naval officers decided they had had enough. They opened the carriage windows and departed, complete with 2 cardboard boxes done up with string, with their names stencilled on them. One was Lt. Parsons, R.N. and I can't remember the name of the other. Their exit was witnessed by some guards who pulled the communication chord, and started firing their weapons, whereupon all the other guards, including those on the blind side, started firing their weapons also. In time honoured fashion all of us started cheering wildly, and those on the off side had a few fleeting glimpses of the subsequent chase, which sadly ended about 20 minutes after it had begun with our friends being recaptured. They decided they had to go into hiding pretty quick and remembering King Charles, thought the best place was a tree. They said afterwards that they didn't have too much time to do this and would be encumbered by their small kit, so when the hunters arrived they were astonished to find, at the bottom of an Italian tree, two packages correctly addressed with their owners in the branches above.

That wasn't quite the end of the story however, because the officer commanding the train decided that to prevent further attempts like that one all our footwear should be removed and locked up under guard until we got to our destination. This sensible act by him became more and more charming as time went on as you can imagine.

Just before we entered Foggia marshalling yards the U.S. army airforce delivered it a fairly shattering blow, and there was certainly no way through for us. We had thus achieved our first 120 miles as the crow flew in 24 hours, and it took several hours more to decide that our next best route to Bologna was via Rome. All the time we were waiting there guards were put all over the place inside and outside the train leaving no way for us to take advantage by escaping. So we set off for Rome by way of Benevento and Caserta, and reached the southern outskirts 24 hours later, to find to our enormous satisfaction, that the brutal British had plastered the marshalling yards just before we got there.

So the Italians had another long pause for thought and decided that we should go back to Foggia on the other side of Italy but before doing so lie up for a day or so in the Pontine Marshes south of Rome. I discovered later that if you were a Northern Italian you reckoned that where Italy stopped and Arabia started was at this very point in the Pontine Marshes. At the time we were there it was July, it was 90 degrees in the shade, with not much shade. It is also where the mosquitoes got into the train, where the flies got into the train, and where everything became extremely unpleasant. There was nowhere to wash, and no way to do so even if there had been somewhere. We'd had our boots and shoes removed. There was plenty of fruit, but not much food and some of us, inevitably, were suffering mal de stomac. So as it happened were most of the others in the same carriage on our train. We were having to use the single loo at the end of the carriage, and the same thing was happening in the single loos at the end of every other carriage on the train. It needs little imagination to understand how the excrement piled up in pyramidical form. It's one of the reasons that even British Rail ask you not to use the facilities when stationary. There comes a time when the top of the pyramid coincides with the bottom of its shaft but whoever is in residence doesn't know at the time that this time has come, nor do his two or three successors. Suddenly there it all is come to the top and it is surprising how the message passes to all the flies. Someone might do some research on that one day.

You might have thought that our guards would have ordered the train to be moved even a few yards every now and then, but they didn't. Eventually our doctor forced them for purely sanitary reasons to allow us to sit out in the field under heavy guard for an hour or so at a time. This broke the monotony somewhat but didn't really help with the stink, because without footwear and after a couple of hundred paces in the Pontine Marshes, we had a new odour to add to all the rest.

As all things will this thing also finally came to an end and the big decision was made that we should return via Foggia, and off we chugged leaving all behind us. Believe it or not, just before we got to Foggia there was yet another enormous daylight American raid on the marshalling yards. Some of their bomb aimers on that occasion however must have been tired as it only took a six hour stop to get things right enough for us to proceed towards the Adriatic coast, and northwards via Pescara. By then we'd been on the railroad for four days and we had run out of practically everything, particularly vino.

My chum Pissy was entirely unputout by such an impending disaster, and recalling the time in a P.O.W. camp called Sulmona where he had been before and was a bit pushed for wine, he had constructed a cocktail made of brilliantine and ink. So he set about luring the Italians into swapping vino for scented soap. In every Red Cross parcel there was one piece of soap. It was odourless soap so that it wouldn't cause any damage to the foodstuff packed in the same parcel. On the outside of every parcel there were printings in various languages like Lebens mittel zur Austeilung - Seife ein stuck. There was without fail ein stuck of seife in every parcel, but although soap was practically unobtainable in the Italy of the time, a piece of odourless soap gave the Italian male or female practically no credit at all. It wasn't being clean that seemed to matter the most, it was being attractive in bed. So Pissy hit on the brilliant idea of injecting with a knitting needle a number of stucks of seife with some of the brilliantine he hadn't drunk. The result was some highly successful pieces of merchandise which he proceeded to exchange for vino all the way up the Adriatic at the stations where we stopped, like San Bernadetto del Tronto, Porto San Georgio, Ancona, Pesaro and so on. By the time we got to Bologna in the evening some 5 days after we had started, we weren't really feeling any pain at all.

It was somewhat of a shock to get reunited with our boots and shoes, particularly as over the period our very smelly feet had also swollen up somewhat and it was a bit painful being marched from Bologna goods yard, because we had indeed arrived in Bologna, to our new camp some way away in La Via delle due Sorelle, the Street of the Two Sisters. We got there and we were searched individually on arrival. They found my escape maps pretty quickly behind the silver paper in a half empty packet of cigarettes, and were very pleased with themselves indeed. And I almost burst into tears to make them feel better. They didn't, however, find my proper escape map which was well hidden in an unmentionable part of my anatomy. So the individual search didn't worry any of us too much. What we were really concerned about were the contents of our midshipman's chests which we didn't have with us.

The camp into which we were put was a very modern barracks, rectangular in shape, with a high brick wall all round, well wired and well provided with elevated sentry posts, bristling with machine guns, search lights and indeed sentries. Our single story quarters were cleanish and not too uncomfortable with three tiered wooden bunks to sleep in, with canvas paliasses which you personally filled with straw as mattresses. There was then plenty of timber around for shoring and facing tunnels in the future, and plenty of roof space around in which to dump tunnel earth, not to mention plenty of canvas on the paliasses to makes sacks to carry the tunnel earth from the tunnel to the roof spaces. It was surprising how they never really learnt, and it didn't take us long to get tunnelling.

Which of course meant that we had survived most of the search of our heavy kit which arrived the next day and was dumped on the floor of a kind of administrative block within our rectangle, and surrounded by guards who were really doing the duty of customs officers but weren't so well trained. This was due to a couple of diversions, one minor and one a bit noisier, organised by an old sapper chum of mine called Tommy Cochrane, who had appeared at Bologna sent from another camp. Both Payn and I had packed our personal chests with great care as described and we each had one diversion packed on the top part. Mine was a short iron bar and Tony's was something else, but we had decided between the dozen or so sewer rats and some of the other tunnellers that we would risk all in putting our major escape tools into two baskets, so to speak, two chests, and so we packed most of the tools into one chest and all of the electrical fittings into another. We shared space between the rest of us to take the personal belongings of the two people who had given up their personal luggage to help with this purpose.

There was no order of march to enter the building where our luggage was. All you had to do was to identify it, take it to be searched and get it marked and cleared. About 20 of us went in together and found our own kit plus the 2 all important chests, and Payn and Cowtan interralia had theirs duly searched. There was the usual excitement when the iron bar was found in mine, and the sound of bayonets being fixed etc. when suddenly there was a violent commotion at the far end of the block which caused the guards and the customs men to tear off down the block to see what was going on. It was the work of a moment to pass the 2 important chests out of the windows at the other end of the block to eager waiting hands. When everything had settled down again we were still fully equipped less the one bar out of my case and whatever Tony Payn had lost. Good for Tommy Cochrane who had fixed it all, and who was instantly elected to become a member of our gang.

It was August 1943 by now, and the Allies were well into Sicily, and it seemed to us that the faster we got out of Bologna the better. We of course did all sorts of reconnaissance including the removal of the footprint end of an Italian style long drop lavatory, because we were quite used to this sort of thing. We settled in the end for a tunnel of the shortest possible dimensions. The place we chose to start from was under the serving counter of our own canteen and where the distance to freedom was only 40 or 50 yards, with only the foundations of the building, the wall and some wire to go under. The soil was sandy and extremely easy to excavate, but being sandy it required proper shoring and lining. As I have said we had plenty of beds. The entry point had to be perfectly camouflaged which wasn⬚t too difficult at all. In fact we had a double entry point, both perfectly camouflaged, one through the wooden floor of the serving counter, and the other via a homemade lid into the excavation itself, which was about 2 ½ foot below the wooden floor joists of the canteen counter. We reckoned that if we went down about 6 ⬚ 8 feet vertically from there, and then started going horizontally with a 3 foot square tunnel that that would be fine and avoid all obstructions. So we got on with it.

Once again we had a gang of 12, 8 of whom were original Padula sewer rats, but sadly we didn't have the services of the like of Jack Occlestone, who had been pushed off somewhere else. We worked in shifts of four at a time, two doing the digging in turn and two removing the earth and stacking it in canvas bags with subsequent distribution in various rafters round the camp. All these and their means of access had to be investigated rather carefully because we were dealing with about 80 - 100 tons of earth for disposal, and you can't just dump that sort of quantity anywhere. Indeed there were other people round the camp probably doing the same thing. It was high summer with lots of daylight and we were able to work for 3 four hour shifts per day. Food was good, there was plenty of fruit and a full ration of vino. Morale was very high as the Allies were advancing through Sicily and up the south end of Italy, so there was everything to gain from getting a move on, and indeed we did.

CHAPTER 15 – ESCAPE AT LAST

We were particularly helped in our means of excavating by the arrival of 2 Italian plasterers who had to do something to the canteen roof, and this had to have scaffolding in order to get at it. The ever watchful Tommy Cochrane, who had become one of our gang as described, instantly knocked all the scaffolding down, quite by mistake of course, with the workmen on top of it. He was most assiduous in helping them to their feet and asking them if they were alright, if they had no bones broken, etc. etc. and during the course of all this, their trowels disappeared. They never reported this matter as they might have lost their jobs, and we had two of the best digging tools for close underground work in sandy soil that could be imagined.

And so it went on without any problems at all until suddenly it became the 8th September, 1943, with the announcement of the Armistice between the Allies and the Italian Government of Marshal Badoglio. The news of this spread like wildfire to such people as ourselves. We optimistically assumed that our guards would pile arms and open the gates, as indeed they did in a number of prison camps elsewhere in Italy from which the inhabitants just walked out. At Bologna it wasn't like that at all. The story goes that the Germans had heard we were armed and likely to put up resistance against their troops who were pouring down from the North towards Naples. Anyway we were attacked in the middle of the night by Panzer Grenadiers with some sort of lightly armoured column, and it was all extremely noisy. In the confusion a few people managed to debunk including T. Cochrane, but all were picked up very quickly, Cochrane by his toes, which were all that were visible of him underneath a pile of rubbish outside somewhere, so he told us.

At first light there were many cries of "Heraus", as we were herded into the 5 yard gap between two 12 foot high barbed wire fences which protected the northern part of the camp from the Italian quarters, and heavy machine guns were lined up on us from guard huts above manned by German troops. I don't suppose there was a single one of us that didn't reckon his last hour had come, but strangely, because there wasn't a blind thing we could do about it, nobody to my knowledge actually expressed this in words, until afterwards that is. We must have been kept there a couple of hours during which time the Germans took over all the guard posts around the camp, and we were herded back to our quarters in exactly the same situation as we were before.

Well, it wasn't exactly the same for two main reasons: the first was that our guards were front line soldiers on their way South and were certainly not familiar at all with the ways of P.O.W's. The second was that the chances of us remaining in Bologna for very long seemed to us to be slight indeed, as we were absolutely dead certain that we would be taken away to Germany by way of the Brenner Pass in no time at all. It was therefore to our utter amazement that we received clear orders from our S.B.O.(Senior British officer) that, with or without caps, we were forbidden on pain of court martial to attempt to escape. We were to cease whatever we were doing and await patiently the imminent arrival of the Allies, and when our guards had left us we were to sit and await further orders. If by any chance anything went wrong we were to move south a bit and report to Castel del Rio Post Office where further orders would be given us. To give him his due he had presumably received these astonishing orders through some means unknown to us, because only a complete madman and blithering idiot could possibly have thought them out all by himself.

Anyway, court martial or not, there were some of us who weren't very interested in complying including, needless to say, the whole of our tunnel gang, but we had to decide what to do for the best. It didn't take us long to make this decision, which was to remain behind hidden in the camp when the Germans marched everybody off. The best hiding place would be our tunnel converted into as big a hole in the ground as possible in whatever time we had available. We were sure there wouldn't be time to complete the tunnel, as even by doing double shift work, and with nothing going wrong, it would have taken at least a fortnight. So we got digging very fast indeed and took considerable risks about the earth removal. We even resorted in the end to using a wheelbarrow with the earth covered over with canteen items such as bottles of vino and packets of lavatory paper. So it wasn't too obvious to our inexperienced guards, who confined themselves to the watchtowers around the walls.

We had to think about how long we would be able to survive in cramped conditions underground, about the supply of air, the problems of attending to the needs of nature, and about the storage of food, water and personal kit. Being under the canteen floor made life considerably easier than having a similar hole anywhere else in the camp, because water supply and drainage was laid on so to speak. We tapped the main for water and tapped the drain to use it as a pissoir. We drilled into the air space under the floor joists to provide additional air, and we jointed in on the electricity supply to produce a light point for use in an emergency. We could also use the space under the floor joists for storage of kit, although this would denigrate the excellence of the camouflage somewhat. So all in all it was quite a project.

The expected blow fell only 3 mornings later and with a lot of noise and cries of "Heraus" the whole camp was ordered to pack up and be ready to leave in 2 hours time. So this was it: decisions before breakfast and that sort of thing. Medical opinion was that our hole could not be used by more than six people for three days, so the first event was to draw lots amongst the 12 of us and get the lucky six down the hole, battened in and camouflaged up as rapidly as possible. This we did in about 20 minutes flat, and as chief sapper on the project, and unlucky in the draw, it fell to me to hide the six away, brush away the dust and finally restore the canteen floor to its pristine elegance. The five other unlucky ones included Tony Payn, John Fane, Tommy Cochrane, Peter Hussey and John Farran, and they meantime held an instant council of war, and decided that the kitchen roof was the place for all of us.

In fact the kitchen was the central part of the same one storey building which housed the canteen at one end and the showers at the other. The only entry point was a door in a vertical wall leading up to the kitchen ventilating windows. We could just reach this door by standing on top of two trestle tables, and we very rapidly formed a chain gang to hoist everything up. There was masses of room up there, in fact it was about 120 ft. long so quantity was no problem at all, and in about ½ an hour we had everything we wanted, including buckets of water, buckets of cold boiled potatoes left over in the kitchen from yesterday, all our kit, blankets and sheets to make ropes from, our pre-cooked emergency rations, i.e. the battle buns that I described before, and last but not least, and very important indeed 22 two litre bottles of red vino, the last of the canteen stocks, because midnight, September 11th, was Tony Payn's birthday, and he had made it abundantly clear that everybody was expected to get pissed on his birthday: he always had.

Our feelings were anyway that we would certainly be discovered by the Germans pretty quickly when they failed to reach the right figure on the final roll call, so we might as well be captured or die in an alcoholic haze as not. Anyway we got some chums in the kitchen to remove the trestle tables, make sure our door was closed properly, and generally remove any tell tale evidence, and we settled down in silence with a bottle in our hands to await events. We couldn't see out of our roof anywhere except later with a complicated system of mirrors. All we could do was to hear, and we heard the final parade being taken about 100 yards away, and we heard the marching feet of 500 or so of our co-mates dwindling into the distance, presumably towards Bologna railway station, en route to prison camp in Germany via the Brenner Pass. We then waited for the expected search and the almost certain discovery. It didn't happen and it didn't happen, and it came on dark and it still didn't happen. The only thing that did happen in our immediate vicinity was the Germans taking over the kitchen below, and making a good deal of noise singing and joking.

Tommy Cochrane, Peter Hussey and John Farran decide to chance it in the early hours when there was no noise from below, so we let them down on sheets and said we would not follow till later to give them every possible chance of getting away. We went on drinking as it really was Tony's birthday by then.

The next thing that happened was noises from the canteen at the other end of the building, and that was the lucky six underground removing themselves and re-camouflaging the hole. Then the pre dawn shift of German cooks arrived in the kitchen for the fruhstuck brewup, so we had missed our chance that night which was to cause us some discomfort and some anxiety later on. However being fatalists we drank a few more bottles of vino towards Tony's health and settled down as best we could for a kip.

During the course of the 20 hours we had been up there and with all the vino we had drunk we kept needing to pee. This of course had to be done silently because of the people below. But it was really very simple as there were several brick dividing walls in the roof and you just kind of closed in against one of those and let it soak into the brickwork. Doing the other thing was a bit more difficult we found, but of course you didn't have to do it so often. This involved getting your buttocks downwards until they touched ground level, then pushing hard, raising the buttocks slowly, moving slightly to right or left, thus avoiding the tell tale plops. We reckoned that it was us who coined and originated the expression of laying a turd – disgusting maybe, but highly necessary and indeed effective.

We reckoned that the kitchen would probably be occupied all day so we decided to make ourselves as comfortable as possible, and selected 3 concrete joists at the canteen end of the roof for our beds. They were about 2 foot wide and as long as we wanted. With a couple of blankets and clothing for a pillow they were really quite comfortable, but you could only lie on your back and had to train yourself not to turn over for fear of falling off onto the ceiling underneath and disturbing the enemy. Also of course we could only talk in whispers. We got rid of our hangovers with an excellent mixture of Canadian powdered milk called "Klim" mixed up with sugar and water, and we contemplated the imminent arrival of the Allies.

We decided that those Allies would drop parachutists to seal off Rome and Genoa and some more somewhere near us, and these would be followed in instantly by sea and air landed troops to cut off the whole of the leg of Italy disposing of the German troops therein piecemeal and of course liberating us in the process. There was something to be said, we thought, for remaining in the roof for a day or two to await these events. It was still summer, we had plenty of food and water and about 12 flasks of vino left. We realised we would have to ration the latter a bit, which would be annoying but sensible. Anyway there weren't any more birthdays coming up. So we lived through the day and waited to see what would happen.

The main thing that happened was increased activity in the kitchen, and the smell of brockwurst and sauerkraut wafting up through the gaps in the door followed by the arrival of large numbers of German soldiers coming and getting it. This went on all night and all day and all night and so on. The kitchen and the camp were never empty and it was obviously being used as a transit camp for front line German troops presumably moving North as fast as they could to prevent themselves being caught by the Payn, Fane, Cowtan strategy.

During one of the days we heard explosives which we assumed to be gunfire and we knew our plan was working and that we would be liberated shortly. We inspected the camp outside with our mirror system and were surprised that the soldiers didn't really look like a defeated army at all, and there wasn't any more gunfire until about the same time the next day. It was all very strange. More and more Germans came through the camp by day and by night, and the kitchen was being operated on a 24 hour basis, so we couldn't have got out even if we had believed it possible. We fell into an easy routine of kipping and contemplating, eating and drinking, listening and looking, whispering and relieving nature as described. Our beards grew longer and our voices got hoarser and our bodies got smellier as we couldn't waste the water supply. We had a cocktail party every evening of 2 litres of vino between us and we didn't have any guests to waste it on. This went on for a total of 11 nights and 12 days. There was gunfire at about the same time every morning which we gradually were forced to admit came from a quarryman up in the hills somewhere. There were an increasing number of Germans but no Allies. Perhaps we thought, but could hardly believe it, the so called Allies had failed to conform to our strategy, and that the Germans were moving south and not north, which led us on to believe that the sooner we got the hell out of it the better. An even more important reason for doing this was that our vino was running out.

There was silence in the kitchen on the evening of the twelfth day, and only very few Germans lounging about in the camp, so we prepared to move, carrying the minimum quantity of kit. We opened the door very quietly, and there was nobody in the kitchen. We had drawn lots to decide the order of march and it turned out to be Fane, Payn and then Cowtan. We made a rope of knotted sheets, we finished off the vino, then lowered Fane with his boots tied round his neck onto ground level. He made a quick inspection, gave the thumbs up sign, and I lowered Payn similarly dressed, except he took my boots with him in addition to his own. I then pulled the sheets up, did a contortionist act to close the door and launched myself into space to grab the vertical steel rod which operated the glass ventilators in the roof. They all clanged shut with a noise of a thunderclap or so it seemed to us, and clearly very instant action was required. The few Germans in the camp square didn't seem to have noticed anything, and when their backs were turned we sprinted in our stockinged feet out of the kitchen door, round the back of the canteen end of the building, and through an open gate in the camp wall. After all it wasn't a P.O.W. camp any more!

We went straight across a wide open field, straight through what seemed to be a blackthorn hedge, straight across a road, then collapsed gasping into some friendly neighbourhood undergrowth. We patted each other on the back, and in our attempts at congratulating each other discovered simultaneously that we had lost the use of our vocal chords. So there we were in the middle of enemy occupied Italy, in our stockinged feet, bearded, smelly, speechless and slightly pissed, but free. We put our boots on. There were decisions to make!

CHAPTER 16 – INTO THE COUNTRYSIDE

We had discussed between us and with others on many occasions what we would do should we ever escape from Bologna, and had really whittled our choices down to two options. They were either to head eastwards towards the Adriatic Coast, steal a boat and head for Yugoslavia hoping to meet the Royal Navy rather than any opposition en route, or to head southwards through the mountains to meet the Allies who would no doubt be advancing rapidly northwards. We had no good source of information or intelligence on which to base a plan and in hindsight we never even considered the bolder options of catching a train, or stealing a car or even a bicycle and heading south that way. From what we heard later one or other of these methods might have brought us success, but I think we were more interested in saving our skins by taking the minimum of risks.

Anyway it was approaching darkness and our first thoughts were to get as far away from the camp as possible as quickly as possible and we decided to head eastwards. This involved the immediate and what seemed to us difficult problem of crossing the main railway heading south. Looking back on it was really laughable the extraordinary precautions we took as though we were expecting soldiers with machine guns all the way along the line. Much to our relief we made it without any incident, and headed into the unknown through cultivated farm land. By about 10 p.m. we were all three very tired physically, and I suppose emotionally. We decided to seek food and shelter.

We happened on a splendid farmer who supplied us with both. It did him the greatest credit to receive into his care without complaint or argument three evil smelling, dirty and bearded rogues, only one of which could speak Italian and that only in a hoarse whisper, and to show us into a fienile, or covered hay barn, and give us bread, cheese, wine and grapes. He was the first of many brave, unselfish, honest, god-fearing government-hating Italian contadini, or peasants, that we and hundreds of others in a similar plight were to meet in the days and months to follow.

We stayed hidden up all the following day and decided, with help and advice from our host, to abandon our plan of heading for the Adriatic, and go southwards down the Apennines instead. So rested, revived, shaven and less smelly we headed for the hills that evening, having thanked our host, still voicelessly, for everything.

This time, not only did we have to cross the main railway line once again, but also Route 9, the Via Emilia, one of the great roads of Italy, but this time with much greater confidence. We had been given bread to take with us and the vineyards through which we walked were heavy with grapes, so we weren't going to go hungry. By early morning we were well into the foothills to the south of Bologna, clearly out of any immediate danger, and in a better position to make decisions about what to do next. We were also well lubricated by the wine we had been given the day before, and all the grapes we had eaten through the night, and also several red tomatoes we had discovered. Our vocal chords were returning to normal. Our bowels were working, rather too freely in fact.

I still had my handkerchief map that I had smuggled into Bologna prison camp, so had the names of the bigger towns and the cardinal points available for general forward planning purposes. But we still didn't know what was happening in the war in Italy, and really had nothing but rumour to go on. Clearly the Allies were still failing to adopt the strategy we had worked out for them, as there was no sign of them round where we were. Nor had the Germans for that matter, though we heard that many thousands had gone southwards, from contacts we subsequently made.

So it seemed to us that we might as well press on southwards as well, keeping to the hills on the Adriatic side of the Apennines, walking by day across country, avoiding major roads and tracks, avoiding towns and villages, holing up by night, preferably in remote farm houses and hoping the natives would be friendly. And God bless them, they were. They practically never failed to offer bread, cheese, wine and grapes and safe, dry cover for the night, either in a fienile as previously described, or in a shed containing maize husks (corn on the cob) and very comfortable maize husks are. Sometimes we slept in beds, and once on a huge stuffed mattress on the kitchen floor with 19 people in it. We weren't the only ones.

We usually left anonymous notes behind describing their selflessness, their bravery and their hospitality, as we were very much in hostile territory, several hundred miles behind the lines as it turned out. In later years, after the war was over, some of these notes were honoured by gifts of a pitifully and miserly sum of money and a message signed by Field Marshal Alexander. It really was disgraceful how badly we treated these wonderful people.

At each place we stopped it fell to Tony to explain who we were, from where we had come, how far we had walked that day, where we were going to and so on. I for one heard what he was saying each time, and gradually learnt it parrot fashion. Of course if anyone answered me I was completely lost, and so, very occasionally, was Tony when they spoke the local dialect called Romalogna. Romalogna was almost incomprehensible even to a non local Italian, so "Da mi da mangiare" or "Give me something to eat" was rendered "Dum dum edet", in their dialect, and all conversations included much sign language to accompany the words or the intent. Thus a slice of bread was accompanied by an outstretched hand, palm downwards, struck with the side of the other hand, indicating the size of the slice. Fear was expressed by the fingers and thumb of one hand held upright, touching and twitching, real fright by the twitching in crescendo; a beautiful girl by the thumb nail being pressed into the cheek, and the partially closed fist being rotated backwards, with the accompaniment of a hopefully lecherous look; a secret by the inside of the digit finger being held against the right nostril, while black market was the outside of the same finger being held against the left nostril, and so on and so on. There seemed to be a sign for everything, particularly for emphasising your point of view, which of course was the only right one in any conversation. We gradually learnt and found ourselves using signs of our own on occasion.

The country through which we were walking was mostly farm land where every inch of ground which could grow arable crops was planted, either with vines, or something else and with some pasture land round the wooded areas. The crest of the Apennines in Emilia and the Marque which is the province south of the Emilia through which we were walking, ran from north west to south east in a general line parallel to the Adriatic Sea from Bologna through Monte Sibilini and the Grand Sasso d'Italia to the Mayella on roughly the same latitude as Rome. This crest could be called the central spine of Italy with ribs running north eastwards towards the Adriatic. Our route lay approximately halfway between the sea and the spine, and therefore it meant climbing each rib, then descending to the south side, crossing the inevitable stream or river at the bottom (not by bridge in case it was guarded) then climbing the next rib.

All the time we never knew quite where we were going, or what we would find round the next corner or over the next hill. We knew where the main towns were and avoided them and we learnt the names of the villages as we went along. We became used to walking two miles for every mile that the crow would fly. We would ask our nightly hosts or any unsuspicious looking passers by how far it was to our next destination, and almost every answer we got, all in good faith, was inaccurate. "2 kilometre, ance de piu, o meno" which means "2 kilometres, more or less", It could easily mean 5 kilometres. "Un hora e mezzo" or 1 ½ hours could easily mean flogging on for the next 3 hours, so life every day was uncertain and full of surprises, but we managed to average around 20 miles a day or 10 as the crow flew.

We were fairly fit, not hungry and rarely thirsty, and now had a quite definite aim in life to get south and meet the Allies coming north. But it never quite worked out like that for reasons we shall see. Since the Armistice between the Allies and the Italians signed on the 8th September, 1943, the whole of Northern Italy was occupied by the Germans. At this time, which was late September, their line was from just north of Naples across to roughly Tameli on the Adriatic.

In this occupied territory the old Fascist laws of the land instituted by Mussolini's regime were meant to apply operating through the regional system down to the local Mayors of the smaller towns backed by the Carabinieri or regular police force. All armed soldiers were meant to remain in their formed units but most of them didn't, and disappeared into the surrounding scenery, some with, but most without their personal weapons. The uniformed units that remained were fanatical blackshirts loyal to Mussolini who was in captivity at that moment, about which I shall explain later. They were loyal to their Fascist masters.

Dire warnings were issued through the system that anyone caught helping or harbouring escaping P.O.W.'s, of which there were many thousands, would be shot, their property burned or sequestered and their families with them. The least that could happen to adults young and old who happened to get caught up in the system was forced labour for the German Todt Organisation concerned with the construction of military defence lands, i.e. pill boxes and the like. It must have been disheartening for the Germans, who did not have sufficient troops to guard their rearward defence lines, to have their defences blown up by saboteurs, partisans and various associated skullduggers soon after they had been completed; but more of that anon.

The individual families up in the hills who gave such unstinting help to escapees had much on their minds to worry about. They had the Germans, the Fascists, the Carabinieri, the local government and possible informers. They hadn't seen any of their huge families and didn't know where they were, whether in Russia perhaps, or Yugoslavia, Albania, Greece, prisoners of war, killed, wounded or in hospital. They just didn't know. They were poor, they were short of food and medicine. The weather could turn against them, the winter was coming. When would it all finish? The higher up the mountains you got, the greater were their problems, but very much greater their spirit. Wonderful people.

One more or less consistent and binding element that existed throughout the web of towns and villages was the priesthood. Mussolini had realised when he came to power in the early 1920's that he must keep the priesthood on his side, and he therefore strengthened the mezzadria system in which the priest was given a plot of farmland, which would be shared with the farmer or owner on a half and half basis, the priest keeping or selling half the produce but not having to work for it. This meant that the priests would go about their business more or less without hindrance with no fears of poverty or starvation. With some very few selfish exceptions this worked admirably and to the advantage of the local communities.

For us escapers these priests were intelligent people with their fingers on the local pulse, the people who you went to for all sorts of local help and knowledge.

We were shortly to meet one in particular, Don Enrico Porcignone, the parish priest of Braccano , near Matelica. We had travelled as described for roundabout a fortnight hearing rumours as we went of bands of partisans beginning to form up in the foothills of the mountains a bit to the south of us, in the general area west of Machurata, centred on the walled city of Matelica. As we got nearer we were directed towards Monte San Vicino, a prominent peak some 4,500 foot high. We climbed towards it with a great deal of circumspection, but fairly soon found ourselves challenged by some fairly hairy customers who turned out to be members of one of the budding groups of partisans whom we sought. This was in early October. Moving on a little bit further we landed up with a bunch who called themselves the Gruppo Roti, established in a farmyard near Roti, which was once the site of an old Benedictine Abbey.

In the next chapter I will tell more about the partisan movement in general and Gruppo Roti in particular.

CHAPTER 17 – PARTISANS, PRIESTS AND RAIDS

After Marshal Badoglio had taken over the government in Mussolini's place much planning went ahead for the formation of the skeleton of a partisan movement to hold the fort in Italy in the event that the Germans did not get out of Italy and withdraw to Germany with the Allies coming up from below. Italy was split up into areas as you would expect, and some form of command structure was put together. We were in the Marque province in Italy. The headquarters of the partisan movement nearest to us was that of the first battalion, prima battalione of the Brigata Mario. It was at Garibaldi Brigade Headquarters in Ancona. As far as we were concerned we had arrived at the site where the Roti group had been or was being formed up, one of three groups around Matelica, the other two being the group called the Erimeta which was located on Monte Gemno which was south west of the city of Matelica, and a group called San Fortunato which was building up in the area of San Fortunato di Porgetto. This was a mountainous area north of the city.

The commandant of the Grupo Roti where we had arrived was a soldier called Lt. Baldini. He was an infantry soldier, called Giuseppe Baldini of the Guides Regiment of Infantry who had recently been part of a battalion which was fighting for the Germans against the Russians. He had got back to his home town of Matelica. The group amongst which we had arrived were a very mixed bunch. There were a number of other Englishmen there, other ranks, including one splendid sergeant major in the Tank Corps called Ginger Davidson who was a great soldier. There were various other ranks from other units who had escaped from other rank prisons, most of them a little bit further south from Matelica in the general area of the Temna Valley. Also there were two Yugoslavs there, one called Jocko, who lived in Montenegro. He was a butcher by trade and always carried a sharp knife with him, a butcher's knife of sorts, and spent a lot of his time sharpening the blade with a faraway look on his face dreaming of when he was going to kill the next German. For some extraordinary reason he had his son with him called Alessandro who was a pilot in the Yugoslav Air force. I have no idea how they got there or what they were doing there but they were both good people and a great help. Then on top of that there were one or two coloured people, Somalis indeed, and there will be more about them later. They had been taken prisoner by the Italians during their war in East Africa, had landed up in a concentration camp near a town called Treja, some way to the East of Matelica, and I will tell you more about that in due course.

So it was a very mixed bunch and Giuseppe was very glad to have Pissy Payn, John Fane and I staying with the group because we brought a great deal of knowledge and expertise to it which the rest of the group did not have. This knowledge was, as far as I was concerned, a very detailed knowledge obviously of demolitions and minefields and explosives and weaponry. As far as John Fane was concerned it was a good knowledge of infantry tactics and the use of weaponry of all sorts. Pissy Payn was not so informed on the military soldiering side because he was an airman, and we didn't have any air force to deal with, but on the other hand he spoke fluent Italian. He was also the senior member of the three of us having become a Flight Lieutenant in the RAF before John Fane had become a Captain in the Infantry, and both of them of course before I was a Lieutenant. I was the junior officer of the three of us. So, Baldini was very happy to deal with all three, particularly Pissy Payn because of his language and because he was indeed the senior chap. He was called Capitano Pyne because that was how they pronounced Payn, but Pissy didn't mind that particularly.

Quite soon we all got to know the priest of the village of Braccano which was about three miles almost vertically down the hill from where we were on the way to Matelica. This was a priest called Don Enrico Porcignone who was youngish, and was very very pro the partisans, very anti German and would do all he possibly could to help the partisan movement at great risk to himself of course. He would appear coming up the hill, with an umbrella in one hand, a cassock gown over his shoulders, and when he opened it up he had a belt with weaponry and grenades stuck into them which of course was entirely not allowed by the priesthood, but he didn't care, and he made his vicarage the Battalion office where we did most of our business. Intelligence arrived from various sources. He had his finger on the local pulse in a big way and there we occasionally met his lady friend, because they weren't allowed wives. Instead of having a mistress, a priest mistress, he had Josefina, a splendid lady, who was the post mistress. It all seemed very appropriate so what with Don Enrico Porcignone and Josefina we were well represented in the village of Braccano. The kind of second in command Italian of the group was a man called Francesco Porcarelli, who in my opinion claimed a lot of credit for a lot of things that he didn't do, but on the other hand he was influential in the city of Matelica and was a good link man to have as an inhabitant of that city when it came to having to do things directly concerned with it.

I think I should emphasise at this stage that the three of us really had no boss whatsoever. We had been ordered by the Senior British Officer in the prison camp in Bologna not to escape on pain of a court martial if we did, and here we were having escaped and beginning to assist a partisan movement. So quite how we would stand in military law should anything happen I have no idea, but we didn't really bother to think much about that. We just set about trying to get the group as organised as possible to help Baldini in his admirable aim.

To this end one of the first things that we had to do was to acquire a lot more armaments than we already had. There were a few Italian rifles about, which were always rather short and never shot very straight. There were a few bombs about, grenades I'm talking about, "bombiamano", and they were pretty ineffective. We didn't have any machine guns and so we really had to think out what we were going to do about it. We were assisted in this by an escaped Somali, who was a prince in Somalia apparently. He was called Aden, a great big, tall, long legged Somali who had got out of the concentration camp near Treja which I have already mentioned called the Villa Spada. He informed us that the guards there were considerably well armed and had, in addition to their own weaponry, an armoury full of weapons which had been handed in or something from the local area, so we decided to raid the Villa Spada.

The Villa itself was some 18 – 20 miles to the East of us across extremely hairy country with nothing but mountains, footpaths and mule tracks. There was no direct route whatsoever, and it was only 5 miles approximately from the German main headquarters in Italy at Mucerata. So we had to make sure that we got there and did our raid during the hours of darkness and got out with our booty, such as it was, in plenty of time to get back into the mountains to Roti. We needed not just ourselves, who amounted to about 20 people, but in addition a bit more help from another partisan band which we found from the place called Val D'Iola. We also needed mules, several mules, to carry the weapons and ammunition that we would hopefully have acquired by then, back to where they were needed with us. So there were quite a lot of plans to make. Then we set off on the evening of the 25th October, 1943. The rain was absolutely belting down and stayed belting down for the whole of our operation, which didn't help much.

Anyway we got to the Villa Spada at just about half an hour before midnight after the most hairy walk in which, amongst other things, Pissy Payn and Ginger Davidson fell down a steep bank where they came off a mule track. Luckily they didn't do themselves too much damage although Payn's leg was going to play up later, and they were able to go on with the operation. The partisan band from Val D'Iola did their stuff in a big way. They arrived at the same time. They cut all the communications emanating from the Villa Spada , things like telephone lines, telephone cables and so on, and when we got there we went over the walls. Ginger Davidson and I were sent off to deal with the Commandant, which we did. We found him and his daughter and we made sure that he took no further part in the operation whatsoever, and P. Payn, John Fane, Baldini and the others rounded up all the guards, disarmed them, broke into the armoury, loaded up the weaponry and ammunition onto the mules that we had with us and after about an hour and a half on the site we headed for home again. We hadn't been attacked by anybody surprisingly, I suppose because the thing was a surprise. Obviously it was to them. Nobody sent out any warnings to the local military, or to the Germans who were only a few miles away, and we set off back on the most ghastly march I've ever done I think, back over those hills and mountains, on those muddy filthy tracks, in the pitch dark, pissing down with rain, but happy and contented and successful. We managed to get back to our camp up the mountain at Roti with our spoils some 19 hours after we had started, and we worked out that during that 19 hours we had traversed over 50 miles of country, and so it was quite an operation. My feet were absolute hell for the next day and a half, what I can remember of it, but I think I slept for most of that time. I was absolutely flogged and so of course were the others, but our tails were metaphorically wagging.

We had acquired enough arms to arm everybody and we had more machine guns than we actually required, heavy machine guns, light machine guns, and the odd hand gun of course that we got off the guards, and one or two sub machine guns too. So it was a highly successful raid, and our little partisan band of Roti became a well armed band. Whether they could use the weapons or not we were to find out by trial and error and practise. I think John Fane was a tremendous help to get all that sort of thing under control.

We were much helped by the local population and farmers. We were always fairly hungry. We had enough food to go round but we had to eat an awful lot of skilley, by that I mean weak brews of macaroni in some sort of broth, and we had very little meat. So one of the things that we did was that Pissy Payn and I, on the advice of Don Enrico, went and called on a prominent ex Fascist who lived on the edge of Braccano who was known to own a heifer. It was suggested that we took this heifer off him, but that we do it in a proper manner. So we called on this guy whose name I can't remember. We said,

"Good morning Signor whoever he was. We understand you have a heifer." He said yes he had. We said, " Where is the heifer?" He said "Well, I don't know why you want to know." We said, "Because we want to take it away from you to eat it." "Oh" he said, "Well I will willingly sell you my heifer." We said, "Thank you very much", we said, "What is the price?" "Well" he said, "It is 28 liras per kilo." The lira of that day was 72 liras to the pound altogether. And we said, "Well Signor, you are a good fascist we understand and therefore you would wish to obey the dictates of the fascist regime that Mussolini has set up." "Oh," he said, "Yes, I am a good fascist and would wish to do that", and we said, "In that case you would be correct in selling us the heifer at 7 liras per kilo which is the government controlled price, and not try and sell it at the black market price to us, is that not so?" He said, "Well I...." We said, "Well, we'll tell you something, either you sell it to us at 7 liras a kilo, and we will agree the weight of it as best we possibly can, or we will shoot you." "Oh," he said, "In that case you will have the heifer at 7 liras a kilo". So we reckoned up the weight of the thing and we multiplied it by 7. We paid him cash for the animal. We didn't shoot him. We said that he had been a true supportive citizen of the regime and "Good morning".

We drove this heifer up the mountain to our camp at Roti and handed it over to Jocko the Yugoslav butcher. We asked him to kill the animal and then cut it exactly in half, to keep one half for us and the group to eat up there, and then cut up the other half in joints so that we could take them down to dear Josefina the postmistress and her organisation to sell the other half on the black market for 28 liras a kilo. This was known as having your cake and eating it Italian style. We of course made good use of the extra money that we had acquired to buy black market goods like cigarettes and tobacco which were very difficult to get hold of, so really everybody was very happy about this indeed.

After this nothing much of note seemed to be happening and the three of us kept wondering when we were going to hear something that was true about the advancement of the Allies up Italy, but this sort of information never came through there, so we knew no more than anybody else. One lived on rumour and hope that the Allies were rapidly advancing up so that we could rejoin them, but this was not to be like that.

So what was happening down in the village of Braccano was that Don Enrico continued to receive information on this and that subject, and there were two items in particular which I will try and describe. One was a report about a particularly nasty man, a baddie indeed, who needed to be pulled in, in case he became a danger to us as an informer. The other came from the station master at Matelica station about the arrival of a wagon including four truckloads of weaponry of one sort or another which was going to become stationary in Matelica sidings. So as far as the first thing was concerned, a partisan called Stelvio Cesarelli and I went after dark to collect this so-called baddie from his village which was about 3 or 4 miles away. We got him and made him get his weaponry out of his haystack and we marched him back to Braccano where Pissy Payn had set himself up as an interrogator. Now Pissy Payn could speak fluent Italian, but he had no idea what he was interrogating this baddie about in particular, so he interrogated him in a very fierce manner in a mixture of very fierce Italian and very fierce German. I think I have previously described on our great train journey from Padula up to Bologna before we escaped how Pissy had made full use of the Red Cross soap to make scented soap out of brilliantine. He knew that was called "ein seife" in German, "seife ein stuck", and he also knew the other bit of German which was on the Red Cross parcels which said 'Lebensmittels fur austilung' which means "food for distribution", and so the combination of fierce Italian and fierce German he scared the absolute wits out of this character we had brought in, and decreed that he should be locked up.

So we marched him up the top to the Roti camp and we lowered him down into a silo which was about 30 ft. deep, a farmer's silo which were underground in those parts of the world. It was, I suppose, not all that airy. It had a hole in the top, so he wasn't going to suffocate, and he wasn't going to starve because we lowered to him the equivalent of a soldier's ration per day as laid down in the Geneva Convention. Uncomfortable he may have been, but safe he was. We got nothing out of him at all, and the awful thing is that it was found out at a later date when we weren't there that he wasn't a baddie at all. In fact he was the opposite almost. So we had got the wrong man, and we had treated him very harshly. However he was heaved up from the bottom of the silo by the partisans who were there when this was found out and he was returned to normal life, possibly slightly the worse for wear. That was a grave error.

On the other information Signor Francesco Porcorelli, who was the second in command of the Roti group as I have explained, did do a good job. He gathered together a small band including Jocko the butcher to go down and raid these static trucks in the railway yard in Matelica, and he found great quantities of ammunition, particularly heavy machine gun 22mm ammunition, which was very useful because we had captured the odd heavy machine gun on the raid on the Villa Spada. There was quite a lot of other ammunition, some of which was of use and some of which wasn't, and some explosive. Jocko had his chance of using his knife, so I believe, on some sentry, who was stupid enough to get in Jocko's way. Anyway Jocko had a satisfied smile on his face when he returned from this particular raid. That was all good stuff, and it kept the morale of this partisan group up. They felt they were really doing something. They were using their weapons and they were beginning to learn a bit about how to behave as soldiers, so it was all good.

Around this time also there was a council of war held in Braccano by various distinguished people from outside to work out what could be done about unloosing and returning the masses of grain that had been sequestered by the Germans and the Fascists. This grain had been locked up in granaries and they wanted to let the population get at it again and use it for themselves and not let it be used by the enemy. To this end the Erimeta group of partisans south west of Matelica who I referred to earlier on and the Roti group got together. They planned and organised to go into the great city of Matelica itself by night and to unlock the granaries, a huge granary there, which was loaded with wheat and other cereals. This actually took place. I took part in this raid. We went up to march on the city of Matelica. There were sentries and things on the gates which were dealt with and the communications to the outer world were cut, so with any luck the Germans in Maturata would not know about this until later. We got into this huge granary and the first thing that we did was load up mule and donkey carts with all the grain that we needed up the hill where the two partisan groups were - all we needed for the future. Having done that we announced to the population of Matelica that they could come and get it, and that we would remain on guard as their guardians of the granary area until 3 o'clock in the morning. Then we would leave them because we had to get back up the mountain before first light if we possibly could. This all happened, and you have never seen anything like what went on there in the middle of the night with the population coming in with every kind of container that they could lay their hands on, load up with grain, and then rush back to their houses and come back for more if they could. There was one particular lady who appeared in her night dress. She was in such a hurry to get there, and she hadn't got a container with her, so she took her night dress off and she turned it into a sort of a sack and filled it right up with grain and with all flags flying so to speak she left the granary in the middle of the night with a sack on her back. A happy lady indeed, and what a marvellous sight she was.

Well we got back up the mountains after this very successful raid and shortly thereafter we had the honour done to us of having mass, a special mass called in the Church in Matelica, as a thank you and a blessing for the partisans who had done it. Some of the local population, also in thanks for the liberation of this grain and other cereals, started sending up the mountain, driven by a strange woodsman in his vehicle, demijohns of wine, a demijohn being a straw covered glass bottle containing 50 litres of wine. So one or two of those came in quite handy. They also provided other goodies, and they also sent up clothes and other things that were going to be useful to the partisans in the winter that was to come. Furthermore we had an invitation, three or four of us, to go to have a meal in downtown Matelica with some of the locals, followed by being led to a house where girls had been provided for us if we wanted. That was something too.

By then it was coming up about mid November and the three of us decided that our time at Matelica must now come to an end. We were not getting anywhere with getting help from the English at that stage, or the Allies of any sort, and there seemed to be no good news of the big advances by the Allies northwards. So we thought we had better move southwards. So the three of us left the group. Ginger Davidson, the tank sergeant major, stayed behind and stayed with them for quite a long time after that, and that is really all I can tell you first hand about our dealings with the partisans around Matelica.

Later on our efforts were very much recognised. I mean very, very much later on, 50 years later, when I was presented with a silver medallion suitably engraved, with lots and lots of tearful speeches going on, and taken round our old hunting ground so to speak, and more or less given the freedom of Matelica. I was able to bring my wife on this occasion, which was only saddened by the death of Giuseppe Baldini, our original leader, the night before the presentation ceremony. He slipped on a marble or tiled floor, where we were talking together, and shattered his leg. He had to go to hospital, because he was pretty weak anyway with a bad heart which had been damaged in the war previously. He was taken to hospital and he died the next day, but I am very happy to say that his son was able to represent him at the ceremony. I was able to present the son with the silver flask that Pissy Payn and I had bought together and had inscribed to present to Baldini. He managed to get it to his father at Talentino where he was in hospital just south of Matelica before he died. When my wife and I called on the hospital the day after the presentation he was still alive and he had this presentation next door to his bed, so he had seen it. So we had a very tearful farewell, and that's the last time I saw this wonderful fellow. But his son lives on and is making great efforts to record everything that his brave father did.

Historically the partisan group stayed together. It got bigger in numbers and scored a number of successes, and it stayed together until the 24th March, 1944, when finally great columns of Germans and Fascist groups came in on the areas around Braccano. Eventually they entered Braccano, they took the priest Don Enrico prisoner, and they murdered him in his own Church in front of his own altar. The German commander of the time refused to allow him to be removed to have the last rites said. After some months I think it was, the family of this very brave priest was given a medallio d'oro, a gold medal, for his bravery during the period between the Armistice and the 24th March when he was murdered. The locals and others who had been involved subscribed to build a memorial, and the memorial stands in Braccano now of Don Enrico Porcignone, and others who were murdered with him at the same time by the Fascists or by the Germans. We have been able to visit that, and there is a picture of it in this book.

CHAPTER 18 - ITALIAN HOSPITALITY

So Pissy Payn, John Fayn and I moved southwards from Matelica in the hopes of finding the Allies coming north from the south of Italy. Hopes were in vain at that time, and fairly soon after we started John Fayn headed westwards toward Rome in the hopes of finding the Allies there. Maybe we had had enough of each other by then.

Pissy Payn and I moved on through Sarnano and Amondala stopping with farmers who risked their lives by looking after us. People told us about a Count who lived in the Commune of Monte Bello and suggested it might be worth our while to call on him, so footsore and slightly weary we found the Count's mansion, rang the bell at the front door and were met by a butler who asked us to wait in the Hall while he got instructions from his master. The Count was obviously an Anglophile because on the rosewood table in the hall were recent copies of the Field and Country Life. This was later made true to see in his library. On the shelf were two books, Les Storie Proprio Cosi by Rudyard Kipling, and Benissimo Jeeves by P.G. Woodhouse.

The Count was very kind, gave us a large martini each and asked us to lunch. We apologised for our clothing and he introduced us to his wife and two younger daughters: the younger of which was a comely lass aged about 20 who wore a tight red sweater stretched across her bosom on which was stitched Dora. (Fullstop). Pissy Payn got to talking to the older sister, and we sat to lunch in the baronial hall – coats of arms, shields, flags and banners, and a footman behind each chair to serve lunch – all this dressed as we were in our strange garb.

After thanking them they advised us to head to Pretare and call on the school which was run in a house owned by the Firmani family. Pretare village is at the foot of a spectacular Apennine mountain called Mount Vettore. We were welcomed by the Firmani family and introduced to the living-in teacher, Rina Torarolo, who hailed from La Spezia. She was a proper Christian, a well educated spinster who had her school rooms at the top of Pretare in the village and following her high principles she insisted that we would be looked after and sleep in the house until further arrangements could be made.

We were given a room half way up the stairs with a large mattress filled with maize husks (corn on the cob) and that was our resting place as long as we were there. Strict instructions were given to the household not to speak about us. The household consisted of il generale, who was an old boy of 75 who had made a pot of money as a miner in Pittsburgh, Pennsylvania like so many other Italians of his age and ilk, in the late 19th Century. He used to sit by the fire in the kitchen leaning on a stick and mumbling, "pork chops, pork chops, whisky, whisky" and so on. He always smiled but had no conversation. I was beginning to pick up Italian quite well, helped by Pissy Payn's translating and by the school mistress with such books as Dickens which I could understand because I would know the English version. She also insisted that I learnt a number of Italian card games like "trestelle" and "briscola" so that in our travels I could play these for money in the Inns en route.

The signora who owned the house did the cooking, laundry and so on. She was the housekeeper in the full sense of the word. She was a lovely old lady and we lived comfortably. I remember eating polenta for the first time, and wouldn't have minded if it was the last . It is made from maize flour, like porridge. It was poured on the tabletop, you were given a fork to cut a portion of the mixture which was ¾" thick or so, and topped with what sauce she had cooked on a trivet over the fire by il generali – rabbit or a bird, or whatever. She also baked bread, using the coarsest grain they could obtain, and an occasional spread of sorts, or possibly cheese. Wine was produced from their own small vineyard and they were allowed one pig on the premises. Every bit was used and stored by hanging bits on wires across the ceiling or on hooks inside the Cinderella hood of the ever burning fire. So we were well fed, and no one disturbed us. When nature called we had signals to say the long drop was free.

We did not leave the house at all except once when I was able to do a wide reconnaissance along the bottom of Monte Vettore to find stretched out for miles the Pinnera Grande on the far side of the Apennine spine south of a village called Santa Lucia. This was originally occupied almost entirely by sheep stealers who rustled sheep and drove them down mountains to Rome for the easy markets there, many years ago. This plain was about 2 miles wide and 8 miles long, as far as I can remember, and was obviously ideal for parachute landings of people or supplies, all of which information I was able later to transmit to the British Special Forces in Sicily when the opportunity arose. I think they knew already.

The time I am talking about was around Christmas, 1943, but it was becoming evident to the owners of the house that our presence there was increasingly likely to become known, and that it would be safer all round for us to move somewhere else. So the son of the house, Fuvio, found that the Commune of Monte Propezzano was such a refuge, and that families there were prepared to accept escaped prisoners as so many other selfless families were doing all over Italy.

With tears in our eyes we moved on foot northwards to the new area which was not too far from the Count. This meant we could continue to meet them and their lovely daughters with great care. The butler had advised the Count that we should come in by the back door and not the front as before!

During the short time at Monte Propezzano we were visited by representatives of the British Special Forces and we helped to arrange parachute drops of clothing, particularly boots, weapons, food and cigarettes, which I have already described elsewhere. We became the receivers of these stores, dropped in brightly coloured silk/nylon parachutes, to be easily visible on the snow if there was any. We made the arrangements to distribute the goodies, and our only real problem was where to put the arms, ammunition and explosive. We solved this by getting the local priest, Pissy Payn's host in the commune, to store these things in the Crypt of the commune Parish Church whenever another body was due to be buried in the commune graveyard. This worked very well. It also meant that as Easter came closer the girls of the village were able to adorn themselves using the colourful material from the container parachutes! In order to give us some income we insisted that their families provide some money into a community pool to help us wanderers.

I lived in a property owned by the best farmer in the village in terms of his expertise and personal strength. This was inhabited by his old wife and by a good looking but thoroughly uninteresting daughter, who they thought would be the right girl for me to marry, and who used to finger my leg by the fire as we kept warm in the early spring months. Always with Dora in mind I evaded her advances. She never knew why!

In this area at the top of the Commune was a hamlet which contained a pub whose owner was the host to two SAS troopers, Jock Murray and Bill Brown. They had been captured in a raid by No. 2 Special Boat Squad on an airfield at the southern tip of Sardinia and had escaped to where they were now. We drank lots of vino in their dwelling, which we could now pay for, and there we learnt the game of La Pasatella with Italian partisans.

Just before Easter a guy called Fausto, who was an Italo/Englishman belonging to the Special Forces, came to collect Pissy Payn to show him the route southwards that we should take when moving on. Pissy Payn was sadly recaptured by local authorities at a road block where an accident had occurred. The Italian soldiers who were trying to sort this out called them in to help and an officious sergeant-major or similar decided to check their identity and discovered that Pissy was an English p.o.w.. He was removed for interrogation (fortunately without torture) to an Italian prison in Ascoli-Piceno and subsequently taken to a P.O.W. camp in Germany.

CHAPTER 19 - SABOTAGE BEHIND THE LINES

I immediately joined up with Bill Brown and Jock Murray up the mountain and we decided to go northwards together to the French frontier to get back to the Allies that way, rather than what seemed like an endless wait for the Brits to come up from the south. We took off north along the spine of the Apennines towards San Sepulchoro and Urbino and came to a village called Varsi in the province of Parma on our famous walk. This, counting all uphills and downhills, was almost exactly 800 miles, completed in 32 days. Bill Brown took off half way to find his own fortune further west towards Rome, which he successfully did, and got home.

On the way we met many partisans and helped them where we could and got much enjoyment out of deceiving the enemy where possible by altering or changing round bridge classification signs. For example a convoy of German ammunition trucks perhaps going south towards the German lines alongside Rome would come across a bridge with a warning sign saying "maximum load 25 tons". We might swap it with the sign for the bridge round the corner which said "maximum load 5 tons". We delayed fairly large numbers of trucks from getting to their destination as quickly as they might have done. Also we were able to instruct local partisans about the last lot of German defences we had seen built on our northern journey, so that they could destroy them when possible. This applied to well constructed pill boxes. These pill boxes always had strong doors put on them with strong locks so that people couldn't wander in and make a mess of them when nobody was in them. Also they had cages inside, presumably to keep birds in, which would give the alarm for gas or anything else. When possible we, of course, reported the exact locations of these concrete palaces so that the local partisans, including ourselves later, could break the doors down and blow up the concrete by using concussion charges inside, which must have been very dispiriting for the Germans, when they tried to occupy them. The pill boxes and entrenchments were built along what subsequently became the Gothic Line, and that incidentally was the last line Jock Murray and I had to cross further west in our later journeyings.

We later found out that the Germans were preparing a new defence line right across the Apennines. This was the Gothic line, which started off near the marble mines on the Tirenean sea coast near Karara. They finished off at what is now a beach resort called Gabico Mare on the Adriatic Sea south of Rimini and in that sort of area. The things that they were building were very strong fortified positions for Platoons upwards to Companies up to Battalions I suppose and also positions for their artillery pieces. They were built by the Todt Organisation with labour which was collected from the villages and towns all around. They used to blow the air raid alarms and the people would flock down to the air raid shelters and they would be picked up to work and labour for the Todt Organisation rather than anything else.

We arrived at Varsi which is a smallish village south of the River Po at the beginning of the Province of Parma and on the eastern boundary of a fairly large and increasingly numerical partisan group whose HQ became the town of Bardi. We moved here and established our own HQ in a requisitioned villa half way up Monte Barigazzo, where hundreds of partisans, mostly youths from towns and villages around Parma and Piacenza, went for shelter and subsequently command and guidance by the Italian partisan group.

The presence of Jock Murray and myself was particularly welcome. We became extremely active in this area and because of our knowledge of demolitions, explosives, sabotage, laying of booby traps and that sort of thing our services were much in demand from the local Italians, who didn't know quite so much about it. We were able to advise and help them with such things – also by devising mines for use on the roads, including a huge mine called the Mina San Giovanni named after me, the inventor.

At this point we knew nothing of D Day or progress in the south of Italy, but on the 6th June, 1944, we woke to find D Day operations had started and that Rome had been captured by the Americans the night before. As soon as the news got through that Rome had fallen and the German armies were retreating northwards the partisan activity in the Apennines in North Italy increased very rapidly indeed. Everybody wanted to get down to it and do the very best they could to do the maximum damage to the Germans while they were in this state.

We had previously helped partisans prepare all the bridges bar one to our mountain headquarters for demolition, leaving the one open particularly to receive wheeled traffic captured on the Lombardy plains on the main areas and installations around Via Emilia, the main east/west road of Northern Italy, near which was Field Marshall Kesselring's HQ at Salso Maggiore. Here there was a huge hospital from which Kesselring removed an ambulance and travelled around the countryside with a Red Cross on top. He was eventually hung after the Nuremburg Trials.

Then, when things appeared to be getting chaotic, presumably because Rome had fallen and there had been an Allied invasion in Europe, all hell was let loose, and we captured quantities of vehicles, food like prosciutto and formaggio, and fuel trailers which we brought up the one safe road for our own use. Becoming increasingly concerned about partisan activity Kesselring said,

"The fight against the partisans must be carried out with all the means at our disposal and with the utmost severity. I will protect any commander who exceeds our usual restraint in the choice of severity in the methods which he adopts against the partisans. In this connection the old principle holds good, that a mistake in the choice of methods in executing one's orders is better than a failure or neglect to act"

Somewhere in his records at about the same time it says that:

"This partisan warfare had its own peculiar aspects, to which the practical rules had to be adapted. Better reconnaissance in the field had to be preceded by early and continuous enemy reconnaissance. The troops were not suitable for this type of work which was reserved for the specially trained security service and the secret field police. The strictest secrecy was essential to the surprise success of any operation. Detailed information of partisan hideouts was no practical use unless they defended it".

It gradually became the rule to cordon off the partisan area and either close in from all sides of the pocket or to attack it with the full troops from a stationary cordon line.

Despite the threat of Kesselring's forces we lived the life of Riley in Bardi, and had many rip roaring parties. The town of Bardi was a prosperous hill city of a spa nature inhabited by rich Italians, many of whom had businesses in London as hoteliers or restauranteurs. So we were never short of money there. We went and asked them for it. They had to be on the partisan side or they would not have survived. There was also one rich Italian family in a local village who owned a great deal of property around in the area. One particular member, La Contessa Sandra, would lend us cars, horses, flats or anything else we wanted. She was all right.

There were various other English groups run by P.O.W's who had been let out of Fontenallato camp rather than having to escape from it, including one group commanded by an Officer of the Royal Tank Regiment called Major Clegg in the area of Ponte d'Olio, who were highly successful in battling various German units who attacked the partisans up the mountains.

I personally at that time was in charge of a radio communication link with our special forces HQ in Bari in Southern Italy where we were able to control supplies of arms and ammunition supplied by the R.A.F.

About the end of July we had been thoroughly discovered, indeed photographed, though we did not know it at the time, by a particularly well briefed and brave German Special Forces man. On having to leave I had to lose my donkey on which the radio apparatus was carried and get myself into safe hiding. Not easy, but we all managed to avoid capture somehow.

We decided it would be wise for us to part company with that group, including Jimmy Corrigan (American Airman) who had joined us having been shot down earlier and who remained with us for the rest of our time in Italy.*

Years later Rose and I visited him and his wife in Woomington, Delaware to their surprise and delight, and he produced a menu on which were the signatures of our group from a restaurant in Rome, where we had subsequently got inordinately pissed.

We moved to an area south towards Borgo Val di Taro. It was in this town one night that some German truck drivers had left their vehicles outside a pub in which we were drinking. Ensuring they were drinking enough we removed their vehicles to our hideouts, and were delighted to find they were full of goodies for German troops further south, such as chocolate, cigarettes, schnapps, and so on. They never knew what happened to the goodies.

Subsequently we moved on to Rossano near a town called Montrelimi, where Major Gordon Letts had formed the "International Brigade of Warriors" as honorary members of the British Special Forces. This Brigade fiercely resisted with great successes the areas immediately north of La Spezia and from which was sponsored an escape line for people like ourselves moving to rejoin the Allies. They were a constant thorn in the flesh of the German occupiers of that part of Italy and were kept supplied by a detachment of British Special Forces such as S.A.S. and others. There was one valley near Rossano called the Zeri Valley which the Germans decided to raid. It was a commune of about 7 small villages who assisted partisans and the Germans murdered everyone in sight. Expecting counter attacks from British forces they poisoned the wine butts in the pubs with cholera bugs "et alia" to the extent that a British Special Force R.A.M.C. doctor was parashot in to find out the truth. He concocted a report which I subsequently learnt off by heart and brought through the lines in my head, crossing lines further south. I did not want to be caught with written papers and therefore hung on a butcher's hook which was a habit of Kesselring's Special Police in dealing with underground opposition. The story of my crossing lines from Rossano follows.

CHAPTER 20 - FREEDOM

We had started our journey near La Spezia in the area of Pontremoli, the Maera and Sarzana and were heading to cross the Gothic Line on our way to and through US Army (5th) positions in the general area of Seravezza and Pietrasanta.

With local assistance we traversed the Appuanian Alps wilderness, overnighting in various marble mines, landing up in one manned by partisans led by an undoubtedly brave and highly operational U.S. Greek army officer. He was in a hutted enclosure – U.S. administrative H.Q. office area in a huge double bed with his beautiful well built lissom brunette mistress ready for anything! Whilst marvelling at the unexpected circumstances and sharing a glass or two with them and my gang I asked his advice as to the best route onward. He had heard on his radio net that the village of Arni had just been captured by the U.S. Army and as it was in the general direction we wanted seemed to be a good route to follow. So in due course, well rested and refreshed, we set off via a fairly hairy route through the mines to arrive in the Arni area the following evening. I went ahead in the dark to recce our next line of march but my first encounter was seeing an armed square headed German soldier outside what was probably his unit's H.Q. So I retreated rapidly and pussy-footed my way back to where I had left the others to plan our further movement avoiding Arni like the plague! This took us westward and southward around another Alp and dawn found us sliding down a rocky scree on our bottoms, rapidly, but in the right direction. At this time we were spotted and shot at from German positions some distance away fortunately with no ill effects or follow up.

Intact and filled with hope and relief we came upon a few houses and scattered villages and poor and bewildered villagers. They helped us with directions and thankfully we came upon Seravezza from the north.

We were advised that there was an Italian partisan band ensconsed in that big house over there (pointing) and they would put us on our best route onwards. The small band of about ½ dozen were in a big lounge room with bottles and bottles of the best red round the walls, and a variety of weapons and hand guns on the floor. They were all drunk and not caring for very much at all taking occasional pot shots out of the windows. Anyway one of them was sober enough to say that our best route could be to go along that stream (pointing) . across that flooded stream . (pointing) . by climbing through the wreckage of a demolished bridge (with reinforcing bars sticking out at all angles) and then to clamber up the well nigh vertical marble gravel scree (like Sisyphus on a good day) to the mine H.Q. huts right up there ..

It was 3 p.m. and pissing with rain but with adrenalin at full tilt we did what they said! The huts were empty but very recently occupied, evinced by a burning Chesterfield cigarette in the manager◻s office. We decided to press on after a short break to recover our breath and dry out a bit. We put out sentries and when we thought the coast was clear with adrenalin doing a yo yo act by now went round the back of the huts and headed for the hills. After about ½ mile down a well trodden track we fell into the surprised but very friendly hands of a unit of the Brazilian Brigade of the 92nd Brigade of the American Negro Division. They, correctly and sensibly, held us as prisoners while they gathered together jeep transport and soldiers to take us down the west side of the mountain to where their Division H.Q. was stationed on the plain by the sea a mile or two North of Pietrasanta.

We were through and free after a long haul!

APPENDICES

APPENDIX I: Mussolini

At this stage in the narrative I thought it might be sensible to put things into some sort of historical perspective as regards the government and the state of affairs in Italy in 1943. Mussolini was born in 1883 in a hill town called Prappio in the Apennines somewhere south of Bologna. He started life as a journalist and slowly became a politician with leanings towards Fascism.

This took him to the Italian parliament of which he became a member in 1921 and he formed the National Fascist Party, and in 1922 he organised and led the march on Rome, and was instructed by King Victor Emmanuel, who was the King of Italy, to restore order after this had been done and to form a government. This he immediately did and became the Dictator of Italy and King Victor Emmanuel was out of the running for many years to come.

In a very Roman Catholic Italy Mussolini, as a Dictator, obviously had to get the Church on his side, and he was able to sign a pact called the Lateran pact with the Vatican in 1929. Later on in 1935 he took part in the conference at Stresa, which was on Lake Maggiore in the north. This was a conference between Great Britain, France and Italy which declared and denounced Hitler's militaristic politics. In spite of this in the very same year he initiated the invasion of Ethiopia by the Italians and the League of Nations approved economic sanctions against Italy because of this. Then in 1936 in July he intervened in the Civil War in Spain in support of the Nationalists of General Franco. Then later on in 1936 in spite of the fact that Mussolini had been part of the conference denouncing the militaristic aims of Hitler he attended a conference which concluded a treaty of alliance between Italy and Germany which was called the Rome/Berlin axis.

Clearly influenced by what Hitler thought of the Jews and what he was going to do about them in Germany Mussolini published the Manifesta de la Razza in July, 1938, which was the start of anti-semitic laws in Italy. Then in 1939 when Germany declared WW2 in September, Italy, in spite of being allied on the Rome Berlin axis, declared non belligerance, so you could never tell with Mussolini what way his politics were going to take him next.

It wasn't until the 10th August, 1940, after Hitler's extraordinary successful Blitzkreig through the Netherlands, and through France and after the withdrawal of all our troops from Dunkirk etc. back to England that Mussolini decided to declare war against England as a full member of the Rome/Berlin axis. Of course he declared war against France at the same time. Great Britain took immediate action to evict the Italians from Ethiopia. They did this with the aid of elements of the Indian Army and of course with a lot of the colonial troops coming up from Kenya and Uganda in the south up into Eritrea and Ethiopia.

While this was going on Italy also put large numbers of troops into Libya to have a large military presence there, and so the majority of Cyrenaica which is the first part of Libya immediately west of Egypt and all the way across to Tripoli was occupied by Italian soldiery from north to south. They became Britain's principal enemy in North Africa in those earlier days of the fighting in North Africa before the Germans came onto the scene with Rommel and the Afrika Korps about a year later. With the occupation of Libya Mussolini then declared that the Mediterranean was "mare nostrum", our sea, and so the large elements of the Italian fleet were brought to readiness and therefore became a special target for the Royal Navy as you probably have all read in your history books.

In the meantime France surrendered to the Germans in 1940 and Great Britain had to make sure that the French Navy were put out of action so that they could not increase the problems in the Mediterranean. This involved the sad task for the Navy of sinking large numbers of the French Battle Fleet in Oran during late 1940 or early 1941. Also during 1940 and the early parts of 1941 Britain had total success in their wars against the Italians in Eritrea and Ethiopia and pushed them all out of there by early 1941 I think it was, so as far as the Italian Army was concerned it was the majority in Libya, no longer in East Africa. This leads me to a small diversionary note.

Mussolini in his dictator-like manner christened his empire in East Africa before he was defeated as "Africa Orientale Italiano", Africa East Italian, and they made a special sort of cigarette to commemorate this great victory and great establishment of the Italian Empire called AOI. Later on when Italy had been totally defeated by everybody the Italians changed the name of that particular brand of cigarette to IOA. That means.... well it doesn't mean anything unless you start off by changing what AOI means which was Abiamo operato in vano, which means "We have operated in vain", and the other way round, IOA, means "In vain we will go on working...."

Historically again of course the USA had come into the war after Pearl Harbour in December 1940 and together with Great Britain had landed troops in North Africa later on in, I think probably early 1942. So the axis forces in North Africa were being squeezed from the West by the American and allied armies and from the east by the British 8th Army together with its allies and by the early part of 1943 all the Italian troops and the Germans for that matter had been removed from North Africa and been pushed back into Europe. So Mussolini no longer had any Empire at all because he had lost East Africa and all his troops in Libya, Tripolitania had been defeated and removed back to their homeland and of course most of the Italian fleet had been sunk by then in the Mediterranean so he had little control of that part of the world any more.

On the 10th July, 1943 the Anglo American armies started the conquering of Sicily and having done that went on into South Italy and on the 25th July, 1943 Mussolini was arrested and put in front of the Grand Concilio. Anyway it was decided that he should be put in prison at the highest point as it was then, the highest prison in Europe in the hotel at the top of the Grand Sasso d'Italia which was the highest point of the Apennines in the Abbuzzi. The government of Italy was handed over to Marshal Badoglio who had been a defeated Italian General in North Africa. Anyway he took off with the government and this was set up in Brindisi on the Adriatic Coast. On the 3rd September Marshal Badoglio signed the armistice treaty with the Allies and this was made public on the 8th September, and on the 10th September the Germans started moving south in huge numbers to occupy Italy.

So there were Germans occupying Italy coming down from the north. There were the Allies having conquered Sicily coming in from the Mediterranean. They started invading the mainland of Italy through the Port of Salerno south of Naples, sometime at the end of September 1943, and Mussolini was up top in his prison at the top of the Grand Sasso, which came to the notice of Herr Hitler, who decided that he should be liberated as soon as possible. He ordered General Student, who had been the leader of the Airborne Forces in the great battles of Crete much earlier on, to liberate Mussolini. So German parachute troops and glider troops together with a special SS commando expert called Otto Skorzeny, made a most remarkable raid on the Grand Sasso d'Italia, and flew Mussolini in a two seater twin engined aircraft in almost impossible conditions from the top of the Grand Sasso to safety in Italy further North. This was a great feat of arms and much admired in subsequent years by people like the SAS, who indeed invited Otto Skorzeny at some later date to have dinner with them at their mess in Hereford.

Mussolini, having been taken to safety, then decided to institute a new Italian government in the North which was called the Republica Soziale Italiano, the Italian Socialist Republic. He set up his headquarters in a town called Salo which is to the south west of Lake Garda half way up Italy and he operated from there supported by Italians who had not surrendered, who had remained loyal to him. They were Blackshirts, and certain unpleasant undercover men as well, and anyway he remained alive until eventually he was captured by the partisans in a fight somewhere up in the Northern lake districts. He was arrested and he was shot, and then he was hung up side down with his woman, his tart, in Milano, so that was the end of him in 1945.

APPENDIX II:
Interview by Peter Liddell

"I have decided to put this interview in full as there is interesting information that isn't in the main story. It is more or less written as told, with a few amendments to make it readable."

P.L: It is June, 2000, and this is Peter Liddell of the 2nd World War Experience Centre, talking at the home of Major General F.W.J. Cowtan, Rectory Cottage, Coleshill near Swindon, with regard to General Cowtan's experience in the 2nd World War which involves the second BEF in 1940 in France and then service in Italy. I don't know yet whether he was captured in North Africa first but I'll learn that soon; escape in Italy, and then service in Northwest Europe. But let's begin at the beginning. Please tell me when and where you were born, and just a little about your family background.

J.C: I was born in West Byfleet, Surrey. My father was in the R.A.F. at the time I was born. He'd just gone into the R.A.F. medical service, having served right through World War I in the Royal Army Medical Corps.

P.L: The year in which you were born.

J.C: 1920.

P.L: Your schooling.

J.C: My schooling – I went to a prep school in Swanage called Forres, then I went to Wellington College, then I went to the Royal Military Academy at Woolwich.

P.L: Did you go to Wellington College with a view to having an army career?

J.C: No. I went to Wellington College because my maternal grandfather was almost a founder member and my mother insisted

I went there and not to St. Paul's where my father went to school, at the same time as Montgomery funnily enough.

P.L: So you would leave Wellington College in 1937 or '38?

J.C:'38.

P.L: And the reason for your having a career in the Army before the outbreak of war – family tradition?

J.C: Well, yes and no. My great grandfather was a Royal Engineer. He was originally in John's Company in India, and then when that packed up he became a Royal Engineer, and he became a full General, name of Kennedy, and so if I was going to join the Army, which I decided I wanted to, I decided to join the Royal Engineers, hence going to Woolwich.

P.L: Well, what memories have you got of Woolwich? It would be necessary I suppose for you to be in Woolwich a little earlier for you to notice any acceleration, any increased seriousness of the course with regard to the impending war. Woolwich would be simply as you found it without the experience of knowing if there were a change.

J.C: Well, Woolwich in August 1938 when I went was beginning to become quite aware that there was likely to be a war, and indeed we went there in August, 1938, and only spent one year there, or two terms at least, not even a year, before getting commissioned in July 1939, instead of having to wait until January, 1940.

P.L: To which field company were you then appointed?

J.C: I wasn't appointed to any then. I had to go and learn to be a Sapper first, because at Woolwich you weren't taught how to be a Sapper - you were taught about mathematics certainly, and physics and electricity and field sketching. You were taught about all sorts of things. You were given a very good background, but you weren't taught anything whatsoever about commanding soldiers, so when it came to commanding wretched soldiers, the soldiers were wretched until their officer began to understand what the hell it was all about. It was not like Sandhurst now where I subsequently went as a College Commander for three years, where we set about teaching people about soldiers right from the start, without actually having any real soldiers to practise on I'm glad to say.

P.L: So on passing out at Woolwich what was the next move for you?

J.C: Well, one went to the Royal School of – well then it was not Royal – the School of Military Engineering at Chatham, where you had to do a course which normally lasted a year to get the groundwork of being a Sapper Officer.

P.L: But in fact in your case you went there in July '39. When did they pass you through that?

J.C: They passed me in January, 1940, so you did six months there instead of a year, and you missed out things like the survey course of it and some other bits of the courses were considerably shortened in order to get you through.

P.L: But I think in fact, despite the fact that you are only I don't know what percentage trained, you would want to say, despite the rawness of your state with regard to the practise of war, you were sent out to the BEF straightaway?

J.C: No, one started off by going to training regiments, or training battalions of drafted soldiers and there you commanded a draft and brought them up, taught them the rudiments of sappery, and we all went and did that for probably a couple of months and I did that at Newark, Notts., during the months of February and March, 1940.

P.L: So when you were sent to France you weren't sent directly to a unit, you were sent as reinforcements as to wherever you were needed. Is that right?

J.C: That's correct. We went by H.M. Ships to Le Havre and we landed up in a place called Forge Les Eaux on the River Bethune approximately. That's the river that comes out at Dieppe I expect you know, and there was a large reinforcement depot there of both officers and soldiers. That is where we went, waiting to be sent to units up the sharp end, but in the mean time the units up the sharp end were heavily engaged, as you know, in the battles which finished up at Dunkirk.

P.L: You haven't explained to me the date when you landed in France because of course until May 10th very little is seeming to be going on.

J.C: Well, apparently understood by the powers that be, whoever they were, the General Staff, that they ought to start sorting out defence lines further west of Belgium and France border, and they decided to put a defence line on this River Bethune, so they didn't have any formed units spare to do this, so they decided to form a battalion of Royal Engineers into a unit called Perowne's Rifles, Royal Engineers, because of the commanding officer, who were to act as the sappers in the preparation of the defence line on the River Bethune from Sirquex which is just North of Forge les Eaux, up to a place called Neufchatel en Bray.

P.L: Now, it may be that I've misunderstood the precise nature of the term reinforcements. I hadn't fully understood as to whether you landed in France before the balloon had gone up, in which case reinforcements would mean something much more innocent than if it had been after May 10th.

J.C: No it wasn't, it was before May 10th. It was in April, and I can't tell you the precise date in April.

P.L: So you were involved in preparing a defence line.

J.C: Yes, yes. I was the adjutant of Perowne's rifles, Royal Engineers, a one off infantry battalion. We were all sappers.

P.L: Well, you were involved or engaged in this work when it was rudely interrupted, I presume, by the balloon going up.

J.C: Yes, absolutely right, yes.

P.L: So, what were you called to do in the emergency?

J.C: We got on with doing just that, getting that defence line organised.

P.L: You stay in the same place?

J.C: Oh yes, we did indeed. I don't know if you've got a map handy, I could show you quickly on the map where it was.

P.L: Are you subjected to interference from the air while you are doing this?

J.C: No, hardly. I don't remember ever seeing any German aircraft at all.

P.L: And how do events in your particular sector develop into the necessity for conceding this defence line and retiring?

J.C: Well, the battles that ended in Dunkirk went on and the Germans obviously probed further westwards after they'd done the encirclement which ended in Dunkirk, and they probed westwards towards Calais, Boulogne, and eventually towards Dieppe and southwards a bit I think to see how they were going to get round Paris, I wouldn't know. All we knew about it was that the odd German started appearing in a reconnaissance manner from the roads from   .

P.L: Now what date would this be, because Calais falls before the end of May, and the last people are away from Dunkirk on June 4th.

J.C: Yes, well it was after that, well across it more or less, a little before and certainly after.

P.L: And how do you get away?

J.C: Well we all eventually went westwards by lorry and by train I think in the end, except the Germans came through our line at Sirquex – I wasn't at Sirquex, I was further back and further North, and according to a friend of mine who was at Sirquex, they captured the bridge over the Bethune at Sirquex intact, by coming across in French armoured cars, with the correct recognition signals and their guns the wrong way round, not pointing forwards, pointing backwards, and when they were over the bridge at Sirquex the guns were pointing in the right direction as far as they were concerned, and that bridge was captured by the Germans intact. That turned the line there to our detriment. I can't tell you much more about it, I was there, but I wasn't actually at Sirquex, thank God.

P.L: Well, let's concentrate on what happens to you and your section.

J.C: Well, I was the adjutant, I didn't have a section, the whole battalion went backwards and we fought no more. They were going to be extracted, I think probably from St. Nazaire. We went as far as there, Pernichet, La Baule, that area where the Lancastrian disaster occurred later, but then they decided they wanted us back to go to Cherbourg to sort out the harbour there and blow up the cranes, that sort of thing. So we got on a train and we proceeded to Cherbourg.

P.L: Got in a train!

J.C: Yes, got in a train, and we went north eastwards. We went back right round the Cote Etain peninsula, to Caen, we changed at Caen, got into some more cattle trucks, and we went to Cherbourg, and we got out at Cherbourg, and we blew a few cranes etc. up in Cherbourg harbour, and we got on a German packet boat, and our commanding officer had to put his pistol in the gut of the Belgian skipper to say get moving, and he got moving, and we went back to Southampton.

P.L: Do you know what date this was?

J.C: Oh, give or take about the 18th, 20th June, something like that. I remember being met at Southampton off this boat by the Women's Voluntary Service, serving up tea. Everybody thought we were heroes, well, we'd done absolutely bugger all actually. But there we were.

P.L: Well, I mean, you hadn't been captured like the 51st division.

.

J.C: Well that's further eastwards isn't it? I was never quite sure how that worked, why that happened.

P.L: Well, let's stay with you. Back to the U.K, reforming, re-equipping I suppose, you must have lost a lot of equipment.

J.C: We didn't lose any equipment. We brought all our weapons back, we lost nothing, we didn't have much to lose. The people who might have lost some things were a splendid lot of Gunners who got back to Brest and then got to Plymouth intact with all their guns, and their commanding officer formed them up and said "You are all members of a new club, and it's called the Left Brest Club. Wasn't that nice? And that was even later, I think that was the 26th June or something like that.

P.L: I must say that's quite news to me.

J.C: Yes. Well we got back to England anyway and then I was posted to the 50th Division – the Northumbrian Division – and our job there was to prepare the South Coast for a state of defence, and my own personal job there was to lay mines mostly between Abbotsbury, Dorset and Swanage in Dorset, i.e. the whole of the Dorset coast including Portland, and to help prepare bits of the Dorset Coast against a possible invasion. It was a very fascinating job, that was.

P.L: Yes, I daresay you would be engaged in that work underneath some of the aerial dog fights of the Battle of Britain as it developed, certainly in August 1940.

J.C: Oh, a full witness of them, wonderful sights in the sky – I mean not wonderful in terms of the poor people who were being shot down, but fascinating to watch from the ground, and cheer like mad sometimes. I remember it very well indeed. Then we had the so-called flap in September, 1940, when the Cromwell code was given out, which I'm sure you know all about. Codeword Cromwell on the 15th September meant that you had to go to your operational positions, and my operational positions were the two bridges, which there were then, one railway, one road, between Weymouth and Portland Bill, and we had prepared both for demolition. The railway bridge doesn't exist any more – there's only one bridge now, but there were two then, and we had them both prepared for demolition with wet gun cotton.

P.L: Of course September 15th is the date when I suppose subsequently it has been decided that the Battle of Britain was won, and so the alarm and the threat of invasion as you have described to me in fact coincides with, to some extent, the end of that threat.

J.C: That's absolutely right, and that's why we weren't in that emergency position for more than two days. We had them prepared for demolition both ends. If the Germans landed on Portland Bill we then would blow them from the Weymouth side, if they landed in Weymouth we'd blow them from the Portland Bill side, and withdraw on Portland. What we'd do then I don't know.

P.L: Is the next career move for you going to North Africa or not? I know there's time yet, but are you then to go to North Africa?

J.C: I'm then to go to North Africa, that's the next thing that happened, but via preparing a 2nd defence line in Dorset, the one that went through Dorchester, quite close to the front defence line, but separated by the cliff area, and then moving north to the Bristol area where we got heavily involved in the bombing of Bristol and having to go into Bristol as sappers and pull buildings down, remove bombs etc., and sort out the water supply for the population and many other jobs. So we did that.

P.L: Have you any particular anecdotal memories of this work in the devestation which hit Bristol?

J.C: I think the thing I remember best was the horrifying business of the George's Bristol Brewery Stables being bombed, and the Drey horses going wild inside and having to be got out. I think that that was really very frightening indeed for everybody, particularly the horses, but for the people getting them out it wasn't much fun either – and the bomb going through the tasting room in Harvey's Bristol Headquarters. It didn't go off, and we went down and got it out and eventually took it out to Avonmouth flats and blew it up, whereupon all our sappers were made honorary members of Harveys, and got absolutely stoned out of their minds daily almost.

P.L: You know when you were telling me about the second defence line. Is this at the time of the building of the pillboxes which still decorate some of our country roads? Were you involved in building pillboxes?

J.C: Yes, I was indeed. It was done by contract, contractors all over wherever the defence lines were, but under the direction of the general staff and the Royal Engineers supervising the construction, and on the Dorset coast, even on the Chisel Bank, pillboxes were built.

P.L: How was it envisaged that these pillboxes would be manned and would play a part in defending communications.

J.C: Well, I can only speak for the Dorset coast bit. About the time of September 15th, and the pillboxes were manned then by the 50th Northumbrian Division.

P.L: How many men to a pillbox?

J.C: Well, it depended on the pillbox, say 2 or 3.

P.L: What sort of weapons?

J.C: Nothing except rifles and Bren guns and Buoys anti tank rifles, which were an absolute waste of time.

P.L: Do you remember - it's very difficult to separate our knowledge today that they didn't come from the spirit of the times, and perhaps you can tell me whether you and your men felt that they would come.

J.C: Well, we felt that they were going to come when we actually had to go and sit on the bridges in a state of waiting to blow them up in September 1940. I   mean why would we have gone to those bridges otherwise? But we did and we assumed that there was going to be an invasion. We didn't see much point in it if there wasn't, if you see what I mean.

P.L: I just wonder whether the destruction that you had seen in France, the refugees and all that was involved in modern warfare, had led to any emotional reaction at the prospect of your green and pleasant land being invaded.

J.C: I think I was too young and too naïve to be worried about it. I mean we were there to do a job. I was a regular soldier but my soldiers weren☒t. They were all TA with the Northumbrian Division, and they had families and so on up in Newcastle. They probably felt about it more strongly than I did. I didn't feel strongly about it at all.

P.L: Because you were professional?

J.C: Well, yes, and I was unmarried, I had no family ties particularly.

P.L: Well, let's come to North Africa. With which unit were you to go out, and what is the state of play in the Western Desert when you go out?

J.C: Well, I went with 50th Division in the 150th Infantry Brigade, and we were the first to go, and we landed in North Africa eventually.

P.L: Where?

J.C: Well we went round the Cape in the Empress of Asia and the Empress of Russia, Canadian Pacific ships, and we landed at Suez, Port Tewfik, and we went up into the desert via Casasine where they gave us three weeks of acclimatisation, I think they called it, or something. We threw away our topees and put on berets instead, and went to war, to start with at Merza Matruh. I'm now talking about April, May 1941.

P.L: Yes.

J.C: And, at that time the British Army had been pushed out of Cyrenaica and had formed a defence line round about the Libyan/ Egyptian border, and our job then was once again laying mines and a defence line going up to the escarpment from the coast roughly at Merza Matruh. We went on doing that. 4th Indian Division were there, it may have been the 5th. They'd come up from Abyssinia/ Eritrea and they were in the defence line, and we the sappers took our orders as sappers from the CRE of the Indian Division, because we didn't have a CRE of our own, because he hadn't arrived. We worked in conjunction with them and a Polish outfit. The Polish Brigade were there then, until the Germans landed in Crete, or soon after the Germans landed in Crete.

P.L: I expect that you were denuded in strength. This greatly weakened the position in North Africa because so many men were sent to......

J.C: Well, we were taken out of the desert, my 150th Brigade were taken out of the desert and sent to Cyprus in a hurry. I say in a hurry, we were sent in HM Ships flat out at night and arrived in Famagusta, Cyprus to put it in a state of defence in case the Germans did a repeat effort. But in fact they were no way in a fit condition to do that. Certainly their airborne people who had fought bravely never fought as an airborne division again after Crete because they got defeated as an airborne unit although Crete obviously was a great German victory. So they never came to Cyprus, but of course we went there to get it in a state of defence. What we did was to prepare the airfields to stop glider landings. We laid a few mines as usual, we were good at that. We were concerned very much with the lack of water on the island of Cyprus to feed a lot of troops. We were concerned with well boring, water detection and one thing or another. We were short of food so our RASC people had to ship cattle and animals from the Lebanon into Larnaca. My job there funnily enough was to prepare landing rafts to take cattle, hog tied cattle, because we couldn't get ships into Larnaca Harbour. There wasn't enough water, so they hog-tied them on board ship and we built big canvas shoots, and these were shot down to rafts which we had made out of local Cyprus boats and very heavy timber, and screaming cattle had come down on their backsides, and we'd unhogtie them, and they'd kick about.....Our early training in Bristol with the drey horses all came in handy, and we landed the cattle that way anyway in Larnaca. It was quite an interesting job. Lot of strange jobs sappers get!

P.L: Yes, I was thinking that!

J.C: Then I had to do an entire demolition reconnaissance of the Island. I was sent off with my reconnaissance sergeant and my driver, and told by the CRE to prepare a plan for the demolishing of Famagusta port, Larnaca port such it was, the railway line which existed then, water supply which was good, or the stuff that we had put in which had to be blown up if we had to get out, and if I had time to go and look at the copper mines and the asbestos mines to see if there was anything we could do about them. That was rather fun, that job. One went from village to village and one got the Muktar and said "We're here for a night, kindly give us lodgings and food and get on with it". So we did that and we prepared the plans for the mining of the panhandle, top right hand bit of Cyprus, the north east thing that sticks out towards Turkey and Syria, and then it was decided that there wasn't going to be an invasion of Cyprus, so we were shipped to Palestine, and 150 Brigade again, although we didn't know it, not us squaddies, junior officers and so on, we were preparing in fact to go to the Caucasus at that stage. The whole of 50 Div. Was going to go to the Caucasus, but at out level, I was a lieutenant, I had no idea I was going to the Caucasus perhaps, and we had no special training to do, nor did we have any special clothing dished out or anything of that sort. And in fact of course we never did go to the Caucasus, but we got into trains and lorries again and went back to the desert. So that's how that happened.

P.L: Captivity for you.

J.C: Well, not for quite a long time.

P.L: Tell me about what happened.

J.C: Well we got back to the desert in, I should think, probably early December 1941, near enough, and at that time we had moved forward and we moved forward and started on the defence line called the Gazala line which stretched as you know from Gazala to Bir Hacheim. At that stage Bir Hacheim was not occupied, the southern defence was 150 Brigade in the Sidi Bahoush box, and the Free French didn't arrive until early May 1942, and I in fact laid all the mines at Bir Hacheim with my section, and had to hand over the minefields at Bir Hacheim to the Free French who arrived from Lake Chad in very good order, including women – that was an extraordinary performance. I was invited to a dance of all things, and I said "Well, I'm not like that". They said, "It's perfectly alright, there are women......" So that was an experience to say the least of it. So that was in May 1942, in the meantime we had been operating very much in battalion groups, they were originally called jock columns, they became battalion groups, all arms, dominating no man's land. No man's land was 70 miles wide then from the Gazala line to where the Germans and Italians were really round Fort Makili, Derna, that sort of area in the foothills of the Jebel. So I was on one very hairy raid in March, 1942, on Martuba airfield. This was a time when they had a very important convoy to get through to Malta.

P.L: Was that Pedestal, the Pedestal convoy or not, perhaps you don't know?

J.C: It may have been, I don't know if it was called that, it may well have been

P.L: I am afraid I should know which month of '42 Pedestal was and I'm afraid I don't.

J.C: Well, I can tell you, round about the 20th March, 1942, is when this particular convoy was going through, and there were 3 main columns from the 50th Division that went right up to and on into the German lines, and Italian lines, in the Jebel Akhdar, and my particular column which was 4th E. York battalion group and a battery of guns and so on had to get into position to shell Martuba Airfield from the ground, and my personal job as a sapper was, because they didn't have a direct line of sight, from the highest point we could get to, they were short of 25 feet of direct line of sight, so I had to build a tubular scaffolding tower, which was 35 foot high, and strap it on the back of a 3 tonner and drive it across 70 miles of desert, or my soldiers did, and erect it on the highest point which had been very accurately surveyed by survey sappers, erected so that the Battery Commander and his OP could go up Jacob's ladder to get to the top of it having had a glass of rum on the bottom. It was very frightening indeed - to direct the shelling onto Martuba Airfield. We were told we had to stay there from when we got there, which was 9 – 10 o'clock in the morning until dark which was about 7.30. We had to stay there come what may and take whatever was served up, and what was served up was an almost continuous bashing from the air. We by the end of it had very little to fight back with in terms of guns. They knocked out the anti aircraft guns, bofors, they knocked out two of the eight 25 pounders and anti tank guns were only 2 pounders on 40's anyway, and they weren't much use to anyone, as of then or later when it came to the real battle. We had 250 odd air sortie strikes on us in that time. Very hairy indeed. But that was the sort of thing we were doing at the time until the battles of the Gazala line which started on the 26th May.

P.L: Roughly when were you captured?

J.C: I was captured on the fifth day of that battle, fourth day of the battle.

P.L: I don't want to get too much engaged in criticism of tactics, still less of strategy, but I have talked to numbers of men, who were not whingers or groaners, but who were complaining bitterly about the way in which they were taken at Gazala.

J.C: Well, I don't know about the way so much as the reasons behind.

P.L: That's really what I ....

J.C: Yes, well as far as 150 Infantry Brigade was concerned, the southern brigade of the 50th Division, who were entirely surrounded and entirely captured or killed, the siting of the Brigade was such that they could not be supported by anybody else. They were by themselves in the middle of nowhere. They weren't in the middle of nowhere quite, they were in the middle of the most extraordinarily complicated mine belts. They were in between two mine marshes, one was called Stepney marsh and the other one was called Hackney Marsh, which I expect you know about, which were enormously wide marked minefields, 3 miles deep, between the forward wire and the back wire with 10 mines per yard of front in between if you worked it out mathematically, i.e. a lot of belts of mine which added up to 1000's of mines. But those mine fields were not covered by fire, and any military man will tell you that an obstacle which is not covered by fire isn't an obstacle in the long run because it can be picked up without difficulty by the opposition. The gap between the 150th Brigade and the 69th Brigade, which was the next one along, or it may have been the 151st Brigade, one of the two anyway, was greater than the guns could cover.

P.L: Well, it's my fault for intruding that point here. I'd like to come to the circumstance under which you yourself were captured, and your reaction to being captured.

J.C: Well, the circumstance was that as sappers in 150 Brigade we spent our life mining, wiring and digging for everybody else but not ourselves, and we had been put in the north east corner of the Brigade box without any mines in front of us and without any wire in front of us and on the day that the German Panzer Divisions came around the bottom of Bir Hacheim and up, came in from the back so to speak, in what was subsequently called the Cauldron I think, near Knightsbridge, we were more or less the first soldiers to be attacked and captured. The reaction was.....we didn't have communications, we had no radio sets, therefore we were not in touch with anyone by radio. We had one two pounder anti-tank gun total defence in our area and three Boys rifles plus 3 Bren guns and rifles, and that was it, and when we sighted the tanks coming, we used our one telephone to Brigade Headquarters and we told them that there was an armoured attack coming in from the north east, and they said, no that's perfectly alright, that's the 20th Armoured

Brigade, and we said they've actually got black crosses on the tanks so it's not the 20th Armoured Brigade, and they said, well, very sorry there is nothing we can do about it. And there wasn't. And we were captured because we had no means of defence, no practical defences, and no weapons suitable for dealing with the 15th Panzer, 22nd Panzer, 90th Light Division, that was it, and we had elements of them that came in on us and we were clobbered. What did we feel? Well, we thought, well, bugger it. Anyway that was it, then we were formed up down in the valley a bit, and we were put in trucks and taken back through the minefield and Hackney Marsh, through which the Germans had cleared because there were no artillery to stop them doing it.

P.L: How quickly were you moved across to Italy?

J.C: A week, 10 days.

P.L: Do you remember your interrogation?

J.C: I wasn't interrogated.

P.L: Which camp were you placed in, or near which town were you placed in Italy?

J.C: We started in Africa, we went to Mimi, then we went to Derna, then we went to Benghazi-Barce, and then from Barce we went to Benghazi Airfield and we were flown, officers were flown, soldiers weren't, to Lece, and we were put in a camp near Bari, which was a transit camp, and from there one or two of us were declared turbulent and we were despatched to the Bad Boy's Camp, the equivalent of Colditz.

P.L: What had you done? Now that was the castle.

J.C: Colditz was the castle, the one we went to at Gavi was a castle, a Genoese castle, yes. A Genoese fort more than a castle.

P.L: What had you done to be thought to be a bad boy?

J.C: We'd laughed at the Commandant. The Commandant appeared at the other side of the wire, and he was wearing a hat which looked like an Austin car badge on it, and he had 4 rows of the same medal for something, and he had creases down the front of his britches, and zip fasteners up the back of his field boots which didn't look right, and we just laughed at him, and pointed, and we were arrested by a squad with fixed bayonets and things and thrown into a cell for a bit and then interviewed by this Commandant fellow about what were we laughing at. I said, "You", simple as that, and he lost his temper and beat me about the face and things with an iron ruler and anyway we were sent off to the Bad Boy's Camp which was for Officiale periculosi e turbulente, but I wasn't periculoso, merely turbulento, and a number of us went off together who had all been laughing at this stupid fellow, and we went into this extraordinary camp..

P.L: Why do you call it extraordinary?

J.C: Because, well, we had never been to anywhere like it before. You entered through a hole in the side of a cliff, through the rocks, down a very steep hill down the other side. There was a 'give up hope all ye who enter here' feeling about it, and you were put in a prison cell when you got there, but the extraordinary thing about it was that all the people in there were all the sort of people you would have liked to have met, i.e. the other periculosi and the turbulenti!

P.L: I think this was the castle from which Jack Pringle escaped. Does that name ring..........?

J.C: Well, he didn't actually escape. Nobody escaped from there. People at the end of the war, at the Armistice some of them, I think 2 of them only got out, the only escape that was nearly made was by a very brave South African miner who dug very deep into the old cellars of the place, and I don't know what. Anyway, because we were turbulente and not periculosi I'm glad to say that we were moved from there and went all the way down south to the monastery at Padula where we tried to get out on several occasions by way of the sewers, and failed at the last moment. We were all moved en block to Bologna, and that's where I got out at Bologna.

P.L: Tell me about that.

J.C: Well, there were 550 officers in the camp and we set about digging as soon as we got there more or less out of the canteen to try and get under the wall and away by tunnel. This was about the end of July, August 1943, and we were getting along pretty well. Then the Armistice came up, and the night of the Armistice which was September 8th 1943, it was clear that the Germans thought we were armed. They attacked the camp and took over the guard, and we were forbidden by the senior British Officer to attempt to escape. Even when the Germans had taken over we were ordered not to escape specifically, and we said "well stuff that". A number of us didn't particularly want to go off to Germany which was quite obviously going to happen. So out of the 550, I think 500 were shipped off to Germany, and I think just under 50 stayed behind in one guise or another. The Germans didn't know how many there were there anyway. They were front line troops that were doing the temporary guarding of the camp.

P.L: Where were you?

J.C: Well, I'd been OC, chief engineer, of the tunnel and there were 12 of us doing the digging and we drew lots and we turned the tunnel into a hole as big as possible for people to hide in, and to have water in and somewhere they could pee and crap and all that and take food in. The doctor said 6 was the maximum, and we drew lots, and 6 went down in the tunnel, and I actually camouflaged them in under the canteen counter, and the other 6 of us looked at each other and three of us decided we'd go up in the roof above where the others were hiding in the hole – this was a modern barracks. We went up into the roof of this place, not expecting to last more than the night at the most before we were found, but we said we would have a go anyway. Nobody found us, but the trouble was that the Germans took the camp over as a transit camp and the only way into the roof was through the kitchen and the kitchen was being used permanently by the Germans to cook up for the transitees 24 hours a day. We were up in that roof for 11 nights and 12 days altogether before we got out.

P.L: You must have had some food and water with you.

J.C: Oh we took everything with us, particularly wine. My real chum was a Flight Lieutenant called Tony Payn and it was his birthday coming up and he said he couldn't remember any birthday when he hadn't got fairly drunk, so let us take wine with us – well we took up 24 two litre flasks of chianti from the canteen and we were very well found up there I can assure you. We took water up. We had Red Cross parcels. We had all the battle buns we had made for escaping, made of chocolate, malt and oatmeal, sugar and condensed milk etc, and we lived very well up there. The only trouble was we couldn't talk except in whispers, and looking after the needs of nature was quite interesting too.

P.L: I was going to ask you about that.

J.C: Right, well it was a modern barracks and there were brick things to hold the roof up, so if you wanted to pee you put your peer up against the brick, and let it out slowly so that it soaked into the brickwork, and if you wanted to do the other thing you put your bum onto the floor, and you lifted it slowly and it didn't make a noise. Simple as that!

P.L: 11 days?

J.C: 12 actually. Anyway when there was no one there we got out and we ran without any boots on through a field, through a blackthorn hedge, we didn't know what the hell we were doing we were so pleased to get out, didn't notice any pain much, and we found we couldn't talk, we had totally lost our voices. We then moved on south in the general direction of... hoping to meet up with the Allies coming up from the bottom, and we had been walking about 2 weeks I guess, perhaps a bit less, when we heard about the partisans forming up near a mountain called Monte San Vicino, and so we went and found them, and we joined them, and helped them. They were just starting. They had no weapons to speak of, except some looted Italian rifles and some hand grenades which were fairly useless, Anyway we helped them to do a raid on a place where we knew there was an armed guard on a camp in a place called Treia, where they were holding prisoner Somalis and other undesirables that they had captured in their Eritrean campaign. We went at dead of night in terrible weather and raided this camp, and killed the guard, raided the armoury, and came back loaded with rather better weapons than we had already, and that was the start of rearming, or arming not rearming, because they weren't properly armed anyway, this partisan group. One heard of, one didn't meet necessarily, of other partisan groups being formed.

P.L: General, you've told me this story as if it were very easy to collaborate with partisan groups. I would guess that it was a good deal harder than that, because they have their own agenda. There were political factors which lead some to support one answer to Italian society, others another. You've got a language problem too, quite apart from personality rivalries. Tell me about working with partisans.

J.C: Well, you're obviously right, but where you are particularly right really came about much later, but at the beginning of the Armistice nobody knew particularly what they were at and politics didn't really come into it. Either you were so pro Mussolini that you would stay with the blackshirts whoever you were, and that might have been 1% of the population, something like that, but the rest of the population were totally anti war anyway. They had been forced into it. They didn't enjoy it, none of the peasants thought about it much, thought anything of it, and politics didn't come into it until much later. When they did come into it then particularly in Reggio Emilia, there was a very strong Communist element and further along the Apennines towards Liguria there was a decreasingly strong Communist element, and they were in it for two things. One, they were certainly against the Germans, anti that, but they were pro themselves Communist, and they were trying to make sure that not only did they remain intact until the Germans finally got out of their country but that they would remain intact very well armed, and most of the arms came care of the Allied Forces dropping them in.

P.L: How long were you to be in association with partisans?

J.C: Well, there was a gap, because Tony Payn had got trouble with his leg which had already been wounded, so we lay up for the winter in the end, then started going north again. He got recaptured and I joined up with two SAS men, and we decided to go up north, and we walked from there up to Liguria. We joined very active partisans there in May 1944, and this was the time when the Germans were fighting the defence line, which was on the River Volturno and Garigliano, down there, before Monte Casino had finished, before Rome was captured. They were still fighting at Anzio, and I think it was probably in that month, May, perhaps it was in April, I don't know, not sure of my facts, that they broke through that line and the Germans came back to the Gothic line which was being prepared from the marble mines of Karara on the west side through to south of Rimini on the east side. On our way through of course we saw some of these preparations which were done mainly by the Tote Organisation. The Italians, the Germans had rastrallementes which means alarm calls where everybody had to report, and when they were surrounded and caught up then they were made to work in things like the Tote Organisation.

P.L: Of course there were some terrible reprisals too for partisan activities.

J.C: Yes, there were indeed. Anyway, at the time when Rome fell, which was on the 5th June 1944, the night before D Day, the day before D Day in Normandy, we were in formed groups of partisans up in the mountains. My group was, I hadn't joined the partisans as such, I had a bunch of English, and we did demolition and that sort of thing on behalf of the partisans. They wanted some expert advice, and we descended from the mountain on the night of the 5th, 6th of June, and created absolute mayhem in the area of S Parma. We blew all the bridges leading into the area where we were which was a vast area of mountains, leaving one open so that we could get vehicles and supplies through from the plain, and created absolute havoc in the area. We removed all the Germans, and we lived the life of riley for about a month and a half before anybody could round us up. We raided out of this secure base. I suppose there must have been about 5000 partisans, something like that, up there. We captured vehicles. We captured petrol tankers and trailers and we took masses of food up with us. We all had cars. We all had horses if we wanted them, women if we wanted them, everything. It was a life of complete abandonment for about 6 or 7 weeks.

Then the Germans had to do something about us because we were a pain in the neck to them, very much so, and Kessering issued some severe orders from his headquarters of Salse Majori, to round this lot up. I was completely in touch with Special Forces then and had radio communication with Bari where Special Forces headquarters was at the time. We had two radio contacts with them per diem, one at 11 o'clock in the morning, and one at 4 p.m. in the afternoon, technically for 2 hours if we could do it with 4 different frequencies in each 2 hour period. We conversed in morse, or the operator conversed in morse, I couldn't do it, to decide what we wanted and things. We sent lists of supplies required in a sort of alphabetical code really. If it was B 1 it meant you wanted another 500 lbs. of plastic explosives or if it was X 2 or something it meant you needed some more socks or boots or something, and you merely put in a shopping list and the special message which you invented like "Giovanni mange lioni", "John eats lions", or something like that. You might or might not get that message through. There was an awful lot of interference, but as we were in the mountains it wasn't very easy for the Germans to come and actually find us as if we had been in a town. Anyway you then listened in to the Voce d'Italia, which was the Allied radio which operated at certain times of the day, ordinary medium wave radio, and you listened for your special message, and if the message, "Giovanni mange lioni", came up it meant that the supplies that you had asked for would arrive at the place you designated within the next 5 nights. You then set up your recconnaisance beacon on your chosen place and with your headphones on you waited for a buzz in your earphones, which meant that the delivery aircraft was within 25 miles of you. You then morse capped at 6 words a minute, very slow, your letters for the day. You confirmed your wind speed and direction by another code to the operator in the aircraft, and with any luck the next thing that you knew is that you had a number of 300 pound containers, 15 if you were lucky, coming down on you, full of goodies. They had to do this, because previously they had to do this Eureka Rebecca (?) business because people had been lighting fires in various shapes, T's and V's and so on until everybody in Italy was lighting fires in various shapes and receiving they knew not what from the skies. And as sometimes this also involved money in terms of gold and rough cut diamonds, things like that, which you needed to pay for goods and services to the peasantry or whatever, these were disappearing into thin air, and they then had to send British Sergeants who'd signed the dotted line, by parachute down with the money instead of dropping it on these strange fires round the countryside where everybody was getting it. Funny life!

P.L: Then you were to be as you put it in a little note to me, captured, this time by an American Division.

J.C: Yes, well, I went on down, I went down to find a very grave officer called Gordon Lett, who had been running a partisan group at a place called Pont Rimini, the Liri Valley, and the Germans had come in and shot up the villages in the Liri Valley, and they had killed the men and the children, raped the women, and all the rest, and they had also poisoned one lot of wine which they had left un shot up with cholera bugs.

P.L: Now, do you know this, or were you told this?

J.C: I know it because I was asked to take a report on it by the medical officer who had done the investigation through the lines. A full written report. I said, well I'm not going to take a full written report of a thing like this through the lines. If I get captured the thumb screws would be even worse than normal, but I will learn it off by heart for you. So my main task coming through the lines was to deliver this report on the German Bacteriological performance to the necessary authorities on the other side wherever they were. So I had this valuable information in my head.

P.L: This is a continuation and conclusion tape being made by Major General FWJ Cowtan of Rectory Cottage, Coleshill, near Swindon, with regards to his wide ranging 2nd World War experience. We've reached on the previous tape a stage when he is leaving the partisans with whom he has been working with an endeavour to take across to the Allied lines information about German reprisal action which surely went far beyond anything which would have been approved by Geneva Regulations.

P.L: But anyway, how did things develop?

J.C: Well we got together – my group was about 12 or 15 strong – we had a guide from, I think it was called, A force, which was an Allied force to help evaders getting through the lines and we headed for the Karara Marble Mines, and we got to the Karara Marble Mines. we said. "What do we do now?", and he said, "we go up and see the boss." I said, "where do you mean we go up?" He said, "you get on that marble lift". The marble lift was a huge bit of metal work with which they lowered slabs of marble by crane down the hill. We had to get on it and be craned up the hill where we met the commander of the partisans who happened to be a Greek officer. We found him at 6 o'clock at night, and he was in bed with his mistress at the time having a gentle glass of something. He said that he had just heard on the radio that the village of Arni had been captured by the American soldiers, the 5th Army there, and he suggested that the best thing would be for us to go through to Arni that night. So we went through to Arni that night. I led the way. I went ahead into Arni myself because I didn't believe everything about the Americans, and the first person I met in Arni was a square headed German with a large bayonet on the end of his rifle what was probably the platoon headquarters or company headquarters or something. So I removed myself gently and said we were not going into Arni tonight. We would have to do something else. So the something else we did was that we went round Arni on the most hairy expedition in the marble mountains, and eventually we crossed the no man's land line on the River Seravezza and went up the marble side on the far side of it in a thunderstorm, 3 o'clock in the afternoon, and arrived in a marble mine manager's office where there was a burning Chesterfield cigarette on the mantelpiece. It was actually burning, and there was about an inch of ash on it. We couldn't make this out at all, we were absolutely flogged and there was a roaring fire in the grate of this manager's office. So I said we would pause for a moment, and put a sentry out to make sure there's nobody else there and dry ourselves out and think a bit. So we dried ourselves out and thought a bit and then decided we'd move on, and we moved on, and the next thing we knew we were taken prisoner by a platoon of Americans. These were the 92nd Negro Division Americans, and the Brazilian Brigade. I never knew the Brazilians fought for us in WW2. Well, they fought for America anyway. They were the Brazilian Brigade of the 92nd Negro Division, with white American officers, who said "Gee, we'd sure like to believe you", and all that, but para.G 235 of our mission orders are that we take everyone prisoners. So I was taken prisoner and so were all my chums, and that is really how we got through the lines. We had the indignity later, I mean I went and saw the commanding general personally of the 92nd Negro Division, and said what a load of rubbish all this was, and why didn't they listen to us. We had just walked through the lines and knew where a lot of the German Defences were. We knew where their medium artillery was, why don't you go and do something about it? He said "well, gee, ... And all this," and we were shipped in an American 5 ton Dodge Trucks open, guarded by American mushroom police with pistols in their holsters all the way to the Allied Interrogation Centre in Florence, where everything got better

P.L: General, would you be kind enough please to take me to the end of your war?

J.C: Yes, I returned to England by way of Naples and was shipped to Liverpool and went on a month's leave, and then I went and did a parachute course at Ringway and joined the 1st Airborne Division, or what was left of the 1st Airborne Division who had come back from Arnhem. I was made 2nd in command of a Parachute Squadron of the Royal Engineers to build it up for whatever the next operation was going to be. There were a whole lot of possible operations, but we were in England and we were the strategic reserve to 21 Army Group, but we were in England, not on the continent. In fact we never went as a formed unit into further battles in Europe until right at the end, in May 1945 by then, when VE Day came. By then I was 2nd in command of the lst Para Squadron RE. We were all sent to Norway and Denmark to take the surrender of the Germans and to lift up the mines. We were back on the mines game again, or to cause the mines to be lifted, and my unit was split between Stavanger, Kristiansand and Copenhagen, so that was a fairly wide front. We got the Germans to pick the mines up until we were told that we were very naughty to do that. We thought it was the obvious thing to do. You got hold of Hauptman Schumach, or whatever his name was, and you said "Good evening, Hauptman," and he said "Good evening, Herr Major", and you said, "Tomorrow, you will pick up that minefield, and when you've done it, you will link arms with your soldiers, and you will walk all over it to make sure that you have got the anti-tank mines up, then you will get into your Kraftwagon and you will drive all over it to make sure you've the anti tank mines up, and he would say "Jawohl, Herr Major" and he would do it. I said he would be looked after by Corporal Jenkins of my unit. It gave the Junior NCO's something to do. It was lovely for them, a great feeling of power, and they looked after the Germans, made sure they did the job properly, and there never was a single casualty. We were told that we were disobeying the Geneva Convention, and this was quite wrong, and we must stop doing it like that and do it ourselves.

P.L: Was your experience in Norway at any stage to lead you closely to the requirement by Norwegians of vengeance against either their quislings or those Germans who had carried out dreadful reprisals against either resistance groups or civilians in general?

P.L: It's an interesting question because my particular unit, the 9th Parachute Squadron, RE, had been on the abortive raid in 1942 on the heavy water things at Bruchen, and two glider loads had been lost on that. One was crashed and got killed and the other crashed and got captured, and the people on board that one were all sappers who were all shot, murdered by orders of Hitler.

J.C:. The Norwegians .... hated the Germans. They really hated them. They hated them more than they hated the Danes I think, more even than they hated the Swedes. They hated the Danes - they had it too easy, and they hated the Swedes, because the

Swedes were neutral, and there the Norwegians were by themselves more or less.

P.L: General, you've given me an absolutely fascinating and informative afternoon. I'm very grateful for your good will towards our work in the centre. Thank you very much indeed.

J.C: Well, it's been a pleasure.

APPENDIX III: Citations

Citation for 1st M.C.: (After the Martuba Raid)

This officer was in charge of the Royal Engineers attached to the Column operating against the Martuba aerodromes on 21st March, 1942. He was personally responsible for the erection of the observation tower which he carried out successfully though subjected to heavy enemy artillery fire. He was continually to be seen in his truck travelling from place to place where the enemy's attack was most intense, arranging and organising his R.E. working parties. His truck was three times hit by cannon shell whilst he was in it but this did not deter him. His devotion to duty and complete disregard for his own personal safety was a marvellous example to all.

Citation for Bar to M.C. (Escape and behind the lines)

As a result of his capture near GAZALA on 31 May 42, Lieut. COWTAN was, at the time of the Italian Armistice, a P/W at BOLOGNA (Camp 19).

By hiding for 12 days in the roof of one of the camp buildings, he avoided transfer to GERMANY, and eventually emerged through a side door of the camp. With two other officers he proceeded to MONTE SAN VICINO, where a rebel band was formed, composed of 14 Yugoslavs and 6 escapers; under the leadership of a Yugoslav, a number of Ethiopian internees were released from TREIA.

Towards the end of Nov 43, Lieut. COWTAN received information concerning an evacuation scheme, and after dispatching all British personnel to the R.V., left with another officer. On arrival at PRETARA he and his companion were prevented by the weather from proceeding further, but during the next three months they made several unsuccessful attempts to penetrate the line. Warned of a Fascist search, they moved to MONTE GALLO, and there assisted another escaper to organise P/W in the area.

In March 44, Lieut. COWTAN participated in an unsuccessful sea evacuation scheme, and after its failure returned to MONTE GALLO. Two months later, intending to reach FRANCE, Lieut. COWTAN and two O.R's went north, arriving at BARDI on 30 May 44. Abandoning their project, they remained with partisans; Lieut. COWTAN played an active part in sabotage operations after first conducting courses in the use of demolition equipment.

Learning of another evacuation scheme on 22 Aug. 44, he went to MONTE REGGIO, but it was not until the beginning of October that he was able to join a party who were guided to Allied forces near LUCCA.

Citation for M.B.E (rescue work carried out at the King David's Hotel, JERUSALEM)

This is just for the record although not part of this story:

On 22nd July, 1946, immediately after the explosion at Kind David Hotel, JERUSALEM, Major COWTAN was instructed to proceed there with his Squadron to undertake rescue work.

On his arrival at the Hotel he found that rescue work was already in progress. This, however, was being carried out without co-ordination, technical knowledge or equipment. Major COWTAN immediately took charge of the rescue work and arranged for work to be carried on continuously by teams of Royal Engineers with assistance from other arms. He organised the clearing of the site and the obtaining of mechanical equipment. Rescue work continued until 2nd August. The work was at all times directed by Major COWTAN and for the first forty-eight hours was under his personal supervision, during which time he was continuously on duty. Throughout this exacting task, which required great determination and skill, Major COWTAN was a source of inspiration to his men who were working under great difficulties and were in considerable danger from falling debris. The fact that many persons were extricated from the wreckage was due to the very efficient organisation built up by Major COWTAN. Without his inspiring leadership and ability, rescue work would have undoubtedly taken much longer, and the number of casualties would have been considerably increased.

ACKNOWLEDGEMENTS

Many thanks to Skye Meredith, Anne Lever and Marcel Cabanes for lots of help with computers, sorting out the commas and generally making this enterprise a little easier.

Lightning Source UK Ltd.
Milton Keynes UK
177353UK00004B/1/P